Fodor's InFocus

FLORIDA
KEYS

T0104144

Welcome to the Florida Keys

Starting in Key Largo, this string of coral islands continues all the way down to Key West, just 90 miles from Cuba. As you head south along the Overseas Highway, with its famed Seven Mile Bridge, you'll find sleepy fishing villages, funky seafood shacks, great snorkeling beaches, and fun tiki bars to take in those legendary sunsets. This book was produced in the middle of the COVID-19 pandemic. As you plan your upcoming travels to the Florida Keys, please confirm that places are still open and let us know when we need to make updates by writing to us at editors@ fodors.com.

TOP REASONS TO GO

★ **Overseas Highway:** This 113-mile road, complete with 42 overseas bridges, is one of the country's most famous scenic drives.

★ **Easy Island-Hopping:** Explore the Upper, Middle, and Lower Keys, from Key Largo to Marathon to Bahia Honda State Park.

★ **Key West:** The so-called Conch Republic is filled with fun bars, restaurants, and shops.

★ **Seafood:** Savor seafood ranging from shrimp and conch to lobster and stone crab.

★ **Adventures:** Snorkeling, golfing, fishing, kayaking, and biking are all on offer.

Contents

EXPERIENCE THE FLORIDA KEYS

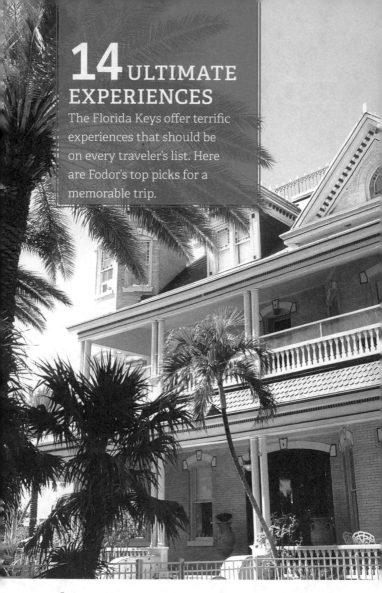

14 ULTIMATE EXPERIENCES

The Florida Keys offer terrific experiences that should be on every traveler's list. Here are Fodor's top picks for a memorable trip.

1 Key West Architecture

Built on stilts to keep things cool, Key West's clapboard conch houses feature porches with gingerbread trim. Many have been converted into atmospheric bed-and-breakfasts. (Ch. 6)

2 Kayaking and Canoeing

Whether you prefer sea kayaking, canoeing through calm and wildlife-rich mangrove waters, or stand-up paddleboarding, the Keys provide the setting and the perfect outfitters. *(Ch. 3, 4, 5, 6)*

3 Key Lime Pie

You're going to need a lot of time and appetite because key lime pie is everywhere, and everyone claims to make the best. *(Ch. 3, 4, 6)*

4 Dolphin Adventures

From watching them in the wild or captivity to getting in the water to swim and interact with them, experiencing dolphins is a classic Keys adventure. *(Ch. 3, 4)*

5 The Cuba Connection

Cuba looms large in Key West, which was settled by cigar-making immigrants. El Meson de Pepe and El Siboney restaurants serve Cuban fare. *(Ch. 6)*

6 Beaches

Keys beaches, including Bahia Honda State Park, Marathon's Sombrero Beach, and Key West's Fort Zachary Taylor Historic State Park, can be beautiful. *(Ch. 3, 4, 5, 6)*

7 Fresh Seafood

You don't have to catch your own to relish the crab, lobster, yellowtail snapper, hogfish, and mahimahi that are signatures of the Florida Keys. You'll find fresh seafood everywhere. *(Ch. 3, 4, 5, 6)*

8 Key Largo's Christ of the Deep

Just outside John Pennekamp Coral Reef State Park on Key Largo, this submerged 9-foot-tall statue makes a divine underwater sight. *(Ch. 3)*

9 Fishing

Jump on a party or charter boat for offshore or back-bay fishing. Or cast a line from one of the Keys' many bridges. *(Ch. 5)*

10 U.S. Highway 1

Despite the traffic, the Overseas Highway (U.S. 1) is an engineering marvel and one of the best ways to to reach the southernmost point in the United States. *(Ch. 3, 4, 5, 6)*

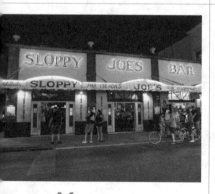

11 Duval Street

Do the Duval Crawl in Key West. There are no rules: stop for a drink, simply wander, or shop instead of drink. But you aren't allowed to go fun-free. *(Ch. 6)*

12 Hemingway's Home

You'll see his name all over Key West, but the best place to start is his historic home, where descendants of his six-toed cats still prowl. *(Ch. 6)*

13 Sunset at Key West's Mallory Square

Not only does the setting sun put on a fabulous show, but local musicians, magicians, and performance artists also join the act every evening. *(Ch. 6)*

14 The Dry Tortugas

Seaplanes and fast ferries deliver you to Dry Tortugas National Park, known for its birding, snorkeling, and historic Fort Jefferson. *(Ch. 6)*

WHAT'S WHERE

1 The Upper Keys. As the doorstep to the islands' coral reefs and blithe spirit, the Upper Keys introduce all that is sporting and sea-oriented about the Keys. They stretch from Key Largo to Long Key Channel (Mile Markers 106–65).

2 The Middle Keys. Centered around the town of Marathon, the Middle Keys hold most of the chain's historic and natural attractions outside of Key West. They go from Conch (pronounced *konk*) Key through Marathon to the south side of the Seven Mile Bridge, including Pigeon Key (Mile Markers 65–40).

3 The Lower Keys. Pressure drops another notch in this laid-back part of the region, where wildlife and the fishing lifestyle peak. The Lower Keys go from Little Duck Key south through Big Coppitt Key (Mile Markers 40–9).

4 Key West. The ultimate in Florida Keys craziness, party town Key West isn't the place for those seeking a quiet retreat. The Key West area encompasses Mile Markers 9–0.

Florida Keys Today

The Florida Keys cater to both international and domestic travelers looking for that laid-back beach vibe combined with modern sensibilities. A focus on eco-conscious tourism and preservation of the environment has led to more sustainable initiatives, while a slew of high-end hotel openings keeps the Keys in high demand as one of the most desirable vacation spots in the country.

SUSTAINABILITY

Key Largo–based Coral Restoration Foundation, the world's largest nonprofit marine-conservation organization dedicated to revitalizing coral reefs, has been restoring eight Florida Keys reef sites, stretching from Carysfort Reef in the Upper Keys to Mile Marker 32 off Key West. In recent years, the foundation reached a milestone with the outplanting of more than 100,000 critically endangered corals, including diverse genotypes of staghorn, elkhorn, and two species of boulder coral.

In 2019 the new Florida Keys National Wildlife Refuges Nature Center opened on Big Pine Key showcasing the Keys' four national wildlife refuges: National Key Deer, Great White Heron, Key West, and Crocodile Lake. Adding to the ecofriendly accommodation options on Big Pine Key is the four-room boutique-style Deer Run on the Atlantic, a Florida-certified green-lodging-program B&B. Located in the heart of the National Key Deer Refuge, the hotel uses organically sourced bedding, supplies, and food, and the property is a 100% plant-based vegan establishment.

LUXURY LODGINGS

The Keys haven't always been known for luxurious accommodations, but that is slowly but surely changing with the addition of new resorts, as well as upgrades to long-time favorites. Ultraprivate, adults-only Little Palm Island Resort & Spa, accessible only by boat or seaplane on Little Torch Key, has reopened with a British colonial design and 30 thatched-roof bungalow suites for a maximum 60 guests. Its dining room now has sweeping ocean views, and its ocean-front pool area offers private cabanas and beach lounge chairs. Hammocks are tucked off crushed-seashell paths.

Another adults-only, luxury property, 12-acre Bungalows Key Largo, is the only all-inclusive resort in the Florida Keys. Its 135 bungalow units average 800 square feet and have private outdoor plunge pools or tubs and cruise bicycles. On-site amenities include three restaurants, two bars, two six-seat floating tiki boats, and a full-service spa with both a Himalayan salt room and a eucalyptus steam room.

In Islamorada, the 214-room, 27-acre, oceanfront Cheeca Lodge and Spa has added a second open-air tiki bar, as well as a zero-entry pool with Atlantic Ocean views alongside a private resort beach. The pool is accessible to all guests and complements the resort's family pool and adults-only pool at the spa. In the summer of 2020, the hotel debuted its Casitas at Cheeca Lodge, 10 villas that offer privacy and exclusivity. The one- or two-bedroom accommodations have large furnished porches, fully equipped kitchens, washers and dryers, and bathrooms with rain showers and large soaking tubs. A Casitas stay also includes personalized butler service.and access to a private beach, a pool, and tennis courts.

Marathon's sprawling Isla Bella Beach Resort and its Key West sister property, Oceans Edge Resort, bring a laid-back feel to Keys luxury. Highlights include multiple pools, cottage-like rooms, and toes-in-the-sand dining.

EMERGING KEY WEST NEIGHBORHOOD

In Key West exciting developments include the revitalization of Stock Island, which locals call "Old Key West." On this small island, neighboring Key West's New Town, you'll find marinas, shipyards, and commercial fishermen.

The cultural scene there now features art galleries, a monthly art stroll where you can meet the artists, and destination restaurants like Hogfish, a popular fish saloon and hangout. New hotels are popping up as well. The industrial-chic Perry Hotel and its adjacent marina offer harbor-view accommodations, three waterfront restaurants, an event space, water activities, and on-site boarding for yacht excursions to view Key West sunsets. The new Oceans Edge Resort is set on 20 acres with both Atlantic and Gulf views. Among its amenities are six pools and the Yellowfin Bar and Kitchen, which serves seafood sourced from the property's very own marina.

What to Eat and Drink

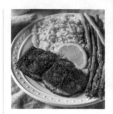

BLACKENED MAHIMAHI

Mahimahi are often caught along the Gulf Coast and served blackened with Cajun spices.

STONE CRAB

Stone crab season runs from October through May, when you'll find claws served at seafood spots throughout South Florida (one of the best is Joe's Stone Crab in Miami).

GATOR TAIL

Just as frog legs have become synonymous with France, alligator has become a Florida specialty. Bite-size, deep-fried pieces are served up as nugget-style snacks and doused with blue-cheese dressing at Snappers in Key Largo. Tastes like chicken.

CONCH FRITTERS

Deep-fried conch fritters may have started farther south in the Bahamas, but this popular appetizer dish (typically served with tartar sauce) has become a favorite in Florida, especially in the Conch Republic of Key West.

MOJITOS

Warm weather begs for refreshing cocktails, so it's no surprise the classic Cuban mojito is referred to as one of South Florida's unofficial drinks. The recipe is easy: a blend of white rum, fresh mint sprigs, sugar, and a splash of club soda.

KEY LIME PIE

Florida's official state pie was first baked in the 1860s in Key West, where local key limes add to the dessert's characteristic tangy taste.

CUBAN SANDWICH

It's said the first Cubano was invented in Tampa, but the sandwich is also widespread in South Florida. It's made with Cuban bread topped with ham, roast pork, Swiss cheese, yellow mustard, and pickles.

CEVICHE

The fresh seafood of the Keys is a perfect match for Peruvian-style ceviche, typically made with raw whitefish or shrimp, lime juice, limo pepper, and cilantro.

ORANGE JUICE

The state's official beverage skyrocketed into a multimillion-dollar industry during World War II. You'll often spot citrus stands just off the highway.

GULF OYSTERS

Slurp down raw oysters sourced from nothern Florida's Apalachicola Bay all over the Keys but especially at Half Shell Raw Bar in Key West, where bivalves are $1 at happy hour.

Best Beaches

SOMBRERO BEACH

Something of a local hangout, beautiful Sombrero Beach in Marathon is worth getting off the beaten Overseas Highway path for (exit at Mile Marker 50 onto Sombrero Beach Road).

SMATHERS BEACH

Key West's longest beach spans the less-touristy South Roosevelt Avenue and is lined with palm trees and has restrooms and picnic areas. Kayaks and paddleboards are available here for a fee, as are beach chairs and umbrellas.

LONG KEY STATE PARK

The beach at Long Key State Park is a typical Upper Keys beach. Rather than a sandy beach, what you see are more like sand flats. If you're willing to camp, you can be lulled to sleep by the sound of the gentle sea waves.

JOHN PENNEKAMP CORAL REEF STATE PARK

A popular stop for snorkelers and divers, this Key Largo park's reef is accessible via boat excursion. And while the park's Cannon Beach is quite small, it's a great place to snorkel from shore.

CURRY HAMMOCK STATE PARK, GRASSY KEY

Picnic pavilions, restrooms and showers, and a playground make this 1,200-foot beach a nice option in the Middle Keys.

DRY TORTUGAS NATIONAL PARK

A fast ferry makes the 2¼-hour trip each way from Key West to the reefs and historic fort on Garden Key. Once there, the snorkeling is fabulous. Campsites are also available for overnight stays.

Bahia Honda State Park

Experience the Florida Keys **BEST BEACHES**

BAHIA HONDA STATE PARK

This state park at Mile Marker 37 holds three beaches, considered the best beaches in all the Florida Keys. They are Sandspur Beach, with long stretches of powdery sand and a campground; Loggerhead Beach, where you can rent snorkel equipment and kayaks; and Calusa Beach on the gulf side, which is popular with families, offering a small and safe swimming area.

HIGGS BEACH

This beach on Atlantic Boulevard in Key West is as urban as beaches in Key West get, with lots of amenities, activities, and distractions. You can check out a historic site, eat at a popular beachfront Italian restaurant, rent a kayak, play volleyball or tennis, or let the children loose at the playground.

FORT ZACHARY TAYLOR HISTORIC STATE PARK

This man-made beach is part of a Civil War–era fort complex and arguably the best beach in Key West, with its typically small waves, swaying Australian pines, water-sports equipment rentals, and picnic grounds.

FOUNDERS PARK

On Islamorada's bay side, this palm-tree-lined beach offers snorkeling, kayaking, paddleboarding, and a picnic area. The beach is part of a public park that also has an amphitheater and an outdoor aquatic center.

Kids and Families

Families who love beaches, snorkeling, kayaking, and sea creatures will revel in the Keys. Although many smaller hotels discourage children, plenty of resorts have kids' programs and activities. Although its wild party scene may seem the least attractive to families, Key West also has family resorts, beaches, and age-appropriate attractions.

UPPER KEYS

Key Largo's **Playa Largo Resort** and **Baker's Cay Resort** offer the best family amenities in a beachfront setting with planned activities. In Islamorada, the atmosphere is more upscale, but **Cheeca Lodge** has always been a family favorite, given its private beach and eco-educational Camp Cheeca.

John Pennekamp Coral Reef State Park on Key Largo provides snorkel and glass-bottom-boat tours, kayak rentals, and safe beaches. In Islamorada, take the kids to **Robbie's Marina** and have lunch at **Hungry Tarpon** before you feed sardines to the truly hungry tarpon. The **Theater of the Sea** entails more marine-life interaction, including touch tanks with rays, sea turtles, and starfish.

MIDDLE KEYS

Hawks Cay Resort, north of Marathon, is a perfect match for families, with its pirate-theme pool, kids' program, and dolphin encounters. For more dolphin interactions, check out **Dolphin Research Center** or **Dolphin Connection**. Families will also feel at home at **Tranquility Bay** in Marathon, where they can play on the beach and spread out in a town house behind picket fences. Don't miss **Crane Point Museum, Nature Center, and Historic Site** and **Pigeon Key** for lessons in history and the environment.

LOWER KEYS AND KEY WEST

Budget at least a half day to spend beaching, snorkeling, kayaking, and hiking at **Bahia Honda State Park**. It's also a good place to rent a cabin. Go in the morning or evening to possibly glimpse the tiny deer at **National Key Deer Refuge** on Big Pine Key.

In Key West, family lodging choices include **The Reach Key West, Casa Marina,** the **Southernmost Beach Resort,** and **Margaritaville Beach House**—all have beach access and are away from the Duval Street hubbub. Casual seafood restaurants such as the **Half Shell Raw Bar** welcome children, and the **Key West Butterfly & Nature Conservatory, Key West Aquarium, Conch Tour Train,** and **Florida Keys Eco-Discovery Center** give families many days' worth of entertainment and enlightenment.

What to Read and Watch

FLORIDA
This collection of short stories by Lauren Groff depicts Florida with equal doses of fascination and horror, dream world and harsh reality. The state is a recurring character, and the diverse settings, cast of characters, and moods give a full and complex impression of the state.

TO HAVE AND HAVE NOT
A desperate Key West fishing captain is forced into the illegal smuggling business during the Great Depression in Ernest Hemingway's book. It touches on the economic disparity in the Keys during that decade and the close but complicated relationship with Cuba.

RAZOR GIRL
A con artist works with detectives to find a redneck reality TV star in Carl Hiaasen's satirical but always spot-on novel, but there's plenty more of his Florida-centric work to choose from (*Bad Monkey*, *Tourist Season*, and *Skin Tight*, to name a few).

THE VEINS OF THE OCEAN
Award-winning author Patricia Engel partially set this 2017 novel, a riveting story of a young woman's journey away from her family's painful past toward redemption and a freer future, in the Florida Keys.

BLOODLINE
Taking place on Islamorada, this Netflix show begins when a bad-seed brother returns home to stir up trouble. A small family inn serves as the epicenter for so much drama it could be a soap opera—full of family secrets, drug trafficking, and speedboat chases.

KEY LARGO
Starring Humphrey Bogart, Edward G. Robinson, and Lauren Bacall, this 1948 film noir classic is about an ex–Army major who travels to Key Largo to pay respects to his late friend's wife and father, who run a hotel on the island. Key Largo now annually hosts the Humphrey Bogart Film Festival in honor of Bogart's acclaimed performance in this movie.

THE ROSE TATTOO
Based on Tennessee Williams's play of the same name, this 1955 film is set in Louisiana but was filmed almost entirely in Key West. In fact, the Rose Tattoo house still stands (as a private residence not open to the public) at the corner of Pearl and Duncan Streets.

PT 109
Warner Brothers filmed this 1963 saga of John F. Kennedy as a PT skipper in World War II, starring Oscar winner Cliff Robertson, at Little Palm

What to Read and Watch

Island—then called Sheriff's or Munson Island and owned by John Spottswood, who was county sheriff at that time. Other action was filmed around Newfound Harbor and the smaller islands, like Picnic and Bird.

LICENSE TO KILL

In the 16th James Bond movie, released in 1989, Timothy Dalton takes the lead role as secret agent 007. The film shows the Seven Mile Bridge and excellent aerial shots of the Keys, as well as the Ernest Hemingway House, Mallory Square, and the U.S. Coast Guard Pier.

TRUE LIES

This 1994 blockbuster film written and directed by James Cameron starred Arnold Schwarzenegger and Jamie Lee Curtis and features the Seven Mile Bridge, which characters drive across while it's on fire (in keeping with explosive Cameron films, it eventually blows up). Filming locations also include Marathon and Key West.

TRAVEL SMART

Updated by
Sara Liss

★ **STATE CAPITAL:**
Tallahassee

♟ **POPULATION:**
71,809

💬 **LANGUAGE:**
English

$ **CURRENCY:**
US $

☎ **AREA CODES:**
305, 786

⚠ **EMERGENCIES:**
911

🚗 **DRIVING:**
On the right

⚡ **ELECTRICITY:**
120–220 v/60 cycles;
plugs have two or
three rectangular
prongs

🕐 **TIME:**
Same as New York

🌐 **WEBSITES:**
fla-keys.com;
keywestattractions.org;
keywest.com

✈ **AIRPORT:**
EYW

Know Before You Go

Where should you stay? Which key is right for you? When should you go? We've got answers and a few tips to help you make the most of your visit.

EACH KEY IS UNIQUE

Key Largo, the northernmost key, is great for diving and luxurious resorts and condo rentals. Its proximity to the Everglades also makes it a great destination for birders; its proximity to Miami's airport makes it ideal for short getaways. Islamorada is known for sport fishing (and for spotting celebrities, particularly those who like sport fishing) and chic resorts with excellent restaurants.

Big Pine Key is perfect for (small-scale) fishing or for kayaking; Marathon is home to Curry Hammock State Park and has lots of midrange accommodations, good food, and great access to water sports, while Bahia Honda Key has the best beaches in the Keys, hands down.

And, of course, there's Key West, known for its myriad attractions—including those for families—night spots, restaurants, and bed-and-breakfasts. It's also the most popular gay destination in the Keys.

LODGING OPTIONS ABOUND

The Keys offer every type of accommodation, from fishing lodges to luxury hotels to historic bed-and-breakfasts. Large-chain resort hotels feature swimming pools, beaches, spas, restaurants, and concierges who will arrange tours and activities.

Smaller resorts have a mom-and-pop feel—some every bit as luxurious as the big-name brands, others ultracasual.

Government incentives to turn headed-for-decrepit historic homes into lodgings have led to Key West's abundance of guesthouses and B&Bs. They range from all-male gay properties and little bohemian enclaves to elegantly turned-out mansions with no luxury spared. Other keys have some fine choices without Key West's crowds and clamor. Some fishing lodges are simple and some more luxurious, with marina facilities on site or close by.

ONE WAY IN (AND OUT)

The Overseas Highway is the only way to traverse the Keys and can often be clogged with traffic, especially on holiday weekends. It's best to avoid peak times like Friday afternoon or Sunday evening, when the four-hour drive from Miami to Key West can easily stretch to six.

WINTER IS THE BUSIEST (AND PRICIEST) SEASON

Rates from December to April are high across the board since most visitors try to escape their own winters, skirt hurricane season, and plan around school breaks. But winter is also the best time to visit, as temperatures, mosquito activity, and water levels (making wildlife easier to spot) are all lower. In September and October, tourism takes a dip and hotel rates plummet.

WI-FI IS THE NORM

Wi-Fi is typically available and often free in guesthouses, lodges, motels, and smaller resorts. That said, it's not always available in every room, especially at properties in older concrete-block or tin-roof structures. The larger resorts often charge for the service.

HURRICANE SEASON SPANS HALF THE YEAR

Florida's annual hurricane season runs from June 1 to November 30. Storms can form within a matter of days, sometimes dissipating or rapidly morphing into monsters. Big storms are more likely in August and September. If you're in or near a storm's projected path, fly out or drive away as soon as possible, even if you're not in an evacuation zone.

BE PREPARED FOR HUMIDITY AND SUMMER RAIN

Florida is rightly called the Sunshine State—and the Keys exemplify this sultry climate. But it could also be dubbed the Humidity State. From June through September, 90% humidity levels aren't uncommon, nor are accompanying thunderstorms. In fact, more than half of the state's rain falls during these months.

MOSQUITOES ARE AN ISSUE

Mosquitoes are most active in the wet summer months but are present year-round due to the state's climate. Although the bugs here aren't typically infected by diseases like West Nile or Zika, humans and pets are still susceptible to their itchy bites.

Pack a repellent or lemon eucalyptus oil to ward off the pests, and wear long sleeves, pants, and socks when spending time in nature. Also, try to avoid the outdoors at dawn and dusk.

SOME SUNSCREENS ARE BANNED

Before you buy sunscreen, make sure your choice doesn't have oxybenzone or octinoxate. These two chemicals, known to cause coral bleaching, were banned in Key West starting in 2021.

Getting Here and Around

Air

The number of passengers using Key West International Airport (EYW) each year is approaching 1 million. Its most recent renovation includes a beach where travelers can catch their last blast of rays after clearing security. You can fly nonstop to Key West from Atlanta (Delta), Fort Lauderdale (United), Miami (American), and Tampa (American, United).

AIRPORTS

Key West International Airport (EYW) is the only airport in the Keys that accommodates commercial flights (Marathon's airport serves charter flights only). Because flights to Key West can be limited and expensive, most visitors fly into Miami International Airport (MIA) and either drive to their destination in the Keys or take an air shuttle to Key West. The trip along the 110-mile Overseas Highway (aka U.S. 1) is long and slow. It can be done in a half day (budget four hours from Miami, five from Fort Lauderdale), but it's better to break up the journey so you can explore more of the Keys.

Key West International Airport is a short drive from Old Town, so should your flight be delayed (it happens often enough), jump in a taxi, head back to town, and enjoy a few more hours of Key West freedom.

GROUND TRANSPORTATION

There are both bus and shuttle services from MIA to the Keys. The Lower Keys Shuttle runs between Key West and Marathon, offering cheap service and multiple stops.

Greyhound Lines' special Keys shuttle departs twice a day (times vary) from MIA's lower-level Concourse E and makes stops throughout the Keys. Fares run from around $25 for Key Largo (Mile Marker 99.6) or Islamorada (Burger King, Mile Marker 82) to around $49 for Key West (3535 S. Roosevelt, Key West International Airport).

Keys Shuttle, another option, runs scheduled service six times a day in 15-passenger vans (nine passengers maximum) between Miami and Fort Lauderdale airports and Key West, with stops throughout the Keys, for $110 per person sharing rides.

FLIGHTS

American Airlines, Delta, Silver Airways, JetBlue, Allegiant, and United provide service to Key West International Airport. (Many other airlines fly to Miami.) Flying time from Miami is 50 minutes, from Orlando just over an hour, and from Atlanta about two hours.

🚤 Boat and Ferry

Boaters can travel to and through the Keys either along the Intracoastal Waterway (5-foot draft limitation) through Card, Barnes, and Blackwater Sounds and into Florida Bay or along the deeper Atlantic Ocean route through Hawk Channel, a buoyed passage. Refer to NOAA Nautical Charts Nos. 11451, 11445, and 11441. The Keys are full of marinas, but they don't have enough slips for everyone. Make reservations in advance, and ask about channel and dockage depth—many marinas are quite shallow.

For nonemergency information, contact the Coast Guard Group Key West on VHF-FM Channel 16. Safety and weather information is broadcast at 7 am and 5 pm on VHF-FM Channels 16 and 22A. There are stations in Islamorada and Marathon.

Key West Express operates air-conditioned ferries between the Key West Terminal (Caroline and Grinnell Streets) and Marco Island and Fort Myers Beach. The trip takes at least four hours each way and costs $130 one way and from $165 round trip (a $6 convenience fee is added to all online bookings). Ferries depart from Fort Myers Beach at 8 am and from Key West at 6 pm. The Marco Island ferry departs at 8 am (the return trip leaves Key West at 5 pm). A photo ID is required for each passenger. Reservations are recommended.

🚌 Bus

The City of Key West Department of Transportation has six color-coded bus routes traversing the island from 6:30 am to 11:30 pm. Stops have signs with the international bus symbol. Schedules are available on buses and at hotels, visitor centers, and shops. The fare is $2 one way.

The Lower Keys Shuttle bus runs from Marathon to Key West ($4 one way), with scheduled stops along the way.

Miami-Dade Transit provides daily bus service from Mile Marker 50 in Marathon to the Florida City Walmart Supercenter on the mainland. The bus stops at major shopping centers as well as on demand anywhere along the route during daily round trips on the hour from 6 am to 10 pm. The cost is $2 one way, exact change required.

Getting Here and Around

Car

Except in Key West, a car is essential for visiting the Keys. The best Keys road map, published by the Homestead–Florida City Chamber of Commerce, can be obtained for $5.50 from the Tropical Everglades Visitor Association.

From Miami International Airport, follow signs to Coral Gables and Key West, which puts you on LeJeune Road, then Route 836 West. Take the Homestead Extension of Florida's Turnpike south (toll road), which ends at Florida City and connects to the Overseas Highway (U.S. 1). Tolls from the airport run approximately $3. Payment is collected via SunPass, a prepaid toll program, or with Toll-By-Plate, a system that photographs each vehicle's license plate and mails a monthly bill for tolls, plus a $2.50 administrative fee, to the vehicle's registered owner.

Vacationers traveling in their own cars can obtain a mini-SunPass sticker via mail before their trip for $4.99 and receive the cost back in toll credits and discounts. The pass also is available at many major Florida retailers and turnpike service plazas. It works on all Florida toll roads and many bridges.

Most major rental companies have programs allowing customers to use the Toll-By-Plate system. Tolls, plus varying (sometimes hefty) service fees, are automatically charged to the credit card used to rent the vehicle. For details, including pricing options at participating rental-car agencies, check the program website. Under no circumstances should motorists attempt to stop in high-speed electronic tolling lanes. Contact Florida's Turnpike Enterprise for more information about the all-electronic tolling on Florida's Turnpike.

The alternative from Florida City is Card Sound Road (Route 905A), which has a (cash-only) bridge toll of $1.60. SunPass isn't accepted. Continue to the only stop sign and turn right on Route 905, which rejoins the Overseas Highway 31 miles south of Florida City.

CAR RENTAL

Unless you fly into Key West and decide to stay in Old Town for your entire vacation—perhaps with a bus trip to another Key or some water-sports excursions—you will need a car. Rentals of all makes and models are available at Miami International Airport, Key West International Airport, and rental agencies throughout the Keys. Reserve your car early during

Car Rental Resources

Local Agencies

Sunshine Rent A Car (Fort Lauderdale)	888/786–7446 or 954/467–8100	www.sunshinerenta-car.com

Major Agencies

Alamo	877/222–9075	www.alamo.com
Avis	800/331–1212	www.avis.com
Budget	800/218–7992	www.budget.com
Hertz	800/654–3131	www.hertz.com
National Car Rental	800/227–7368	www.nationalcar.com

big events such as Homestead-Miami Speedway races (Key Largo is often affected), October's Fantasy Fest in Key West, and the Christmas and Easter holidays.

It's usually cheaper to rent in either Fort Lauderdale or Miami if you are driving down from one of those airports. ■TIP→ Avoid flying into Key West and driving back to Miami; there could be substantial drop-off charges for leaving a Key West car there.

GASOLINE

The deeper you go into the Keys, the higher the pump price goes. Gas stations in Homestead and Florida City have some of the most affordable prices in South Florida, so fill your tank in Miami and top it off in Florida City.

MILE MARKERS

Getting lost in the Keys is almost impossible once you understand the unique address system. Many addresses are simply given as a mile marker (MM) number. The markers are small, green, rectangular signs along the side of the Overseas Highway (U.S. 1). They begin with Mile Marker 126, 1 mile south of Florida City, and end with Mile Marker 0, in Key West. Keys residents use the abbreviation BS for the bay side of Overseas Highway and OS for the ocean side. From Marathon to Key West, residents may refer to the bay side as the gulf side.

PARKING

The only place where parking is a problem is in Old Town in Key West. There are public parking lots that charge by the day (some hotels and B&Bs

Getting Here and Around

provide parking or discounts at municipal lots). If you arrive early, you can sometimes find spots on side streets off Duval and Whitehead, where you can park for free—just be sure it's not marked for residential parking only.

If you don't want to walk around town, your best bet is to bike or take a trolley, which lets you hop on and hop off at several different stops. The Conch Tour Train makes only two stops where you can board and disembark.

ROAD CONDITIONS

Most of the Overseas Highway is narrow and busy, especially on weekends and in high season. Expect delays behind RVs, trucks, cars towing boats, and rubbernecking tourists. The section of highway that travels from the mainland to Key Largo is particularly slow and congested. Occasional passing lanes allow you to get past slow-moving trucks. The quality of local roads in Key West is good, though some side streets are narrow. Traffic in the historic district often becomes congested throughout the day and night.

 Taxi

Key Lime Taxi operates around the clock in Key West. The fare for two or more from the Key West airport to Old Town is $9 per person. Otherwise, meters register $2.95 for the first 1/5 mile, $8 per mile.

Essentials

Activities

The Keys are all about being on and in the water. Good visibility, vibrant reefs, and abundant sea life make diving especially popular. Dive shops up and down the Overseas Highway offer trips, instruction, and equipment. The fishing here is spectacular, too, attracting the rod-and-reel crowd in search of big game such as marlin, tarpon, and mahimahi as well as flats dwellers, most notably the easily spooked bonefish.

On land, exploring Key West is the most popular pastime. Visitors do the "Duval Crawl" through the pubs and bars of Old Town. On its fringes, the island holds some of the Keys' best beaches, although they are all man-made. For a more serious crowd, plenty of museums, galleries, and historic sights offer cultural stimulation.

Health
COVID-19

Most travel restrictions, including vaccination and masking requirements, have been lifted across the United States except in healthcare facilities and nursing homes. Some travelers may still wish to wear a mask in confined spaces, including on airplanes, on public transportation, and at large indoor gatherings, but that is increasingly a personal choice. Be aware that some local mandates still exist and should be followed.

Hotels

There are plenty of franchised operations and major-chain destination resorts, but intimate lodging—small, sometimes family-owned guesthouses and fishing lodges—is characteristic of the Keys. This is particularly true in Key West's Old Town, where many historic Victorian homes have been transformed into B&Bs. Most serve only continental breakfast (a restaurant license is required to serve hot food).

Hotels and other lodgings generally require you to give your credit-card details before they will confirm your reservation. If you don't feel comfortable emailing this information, ask if you can fax it (some places even prefer faxes). However you book, get confirmation in writing, and have a copy of it handy when you check in.

Be sure you understand the hotel's cancellation policy. Some places allow you to cancel without any kind of

Essentials

penalty—even if you prepaid to secure a discounted rate—if you cancel at least 24 hours in advance. Others require you to cancel a week in advance or penalize you the cost of one night. Small inns and B&Bs are most likely to require you to cancel far in advance.

Most hotels allow children under a certain age to stay in their parents' room at no extra charge, but others charge for them as extra adults; find out the cutoff age for discounts. Many of Key West's guesthouses do not allow children under a certain age.

APARTMENT AND HOUSE RENTALS

Although short-term rentals are available throughout the Keys, Key West has the largest inventory, and several rental companies can hook you up. (See Lodging Alternatives in the Key West chapter for local vacation-rental agencies.) Airbnb (⊕ www.airbnb.com) and VRBO (⊕ www.vrbo.com) are also good resources for finding a vacation rental in the Keys.

Throughout this guide, hotel reviews have been shortened. For full information, visit Fodors.com. Hotel prices cited are the lowest cost of a standard double room in high season.

What It Costs

$	$$	$$$	$$$$
FOR TWO PEOPLE			
under $200	$200–$300	$301–$400	over $400

🍴 Restaurants

Although the Keys have a good variety of restaurants, most people rave about the colorful seaside fish houses, some of which more character than others. The seafood is so fresh—especially local catches of snapper, mahimahi, grouper, lobster, and stone—that you'll be spoiled for life. Florida spiny lobster season runs from August to March and that for stone crabs is from mid-October to mid-May.

Keep an eye out for authentic key lime pie. The real McCoy has yellow filling in a graham-cracker crust and tastes pleasantly tart. (If it's green, just say no.) Bahamian and Cuban styles influence local cuisine, so try to sample some conch fritters and black beans and rice.

Restaurants might close for a two- to four-week vacation during the slow season—between mid-September and mid-November. *Throughout this guide, restaurant reviews have been shortened. For full information visit Fodors.com.*

MEALS AND MEALTIMES

Unless otherwise noted, the restaurants listed in this guide are open daily for lunch and dinner.

PAYING

Most restaurants accept major credit cards. Some of the small, family-owned operations do not. *Restaurant prices cited throughout this guide are the average cost of a main course at dinner, or if dinner is not served, at lunch.*

RESERVATIONS AND DRESS

It's a good idea to make a reservation if you can. We only mention them specifically when reservations are essential or not accepted. For popular restaurants, book as far ahead as possible and reconfirm as soon as you arrive. (Large parties should always call ahead to check the reservations policy.) Online reservation services make it easy to book a table before you even leave home.

WINE, BEER, AND SPIRITS

If the Keys have a representative tipple, it is the margarita. Several microbreweries have also popped up in recent years.

What It Costs			
$	$$	$$$	$$$$
AT DINNER			
under $20	$20–$25	$26–$35	over $35

💲 Tipping

In restaurants, a tip of 18% of the tab is sufficient except at the fanciest, most expensive places, where a larger tip of around 20% is more common. It's common courtesy to leave a dollar or two per night for the housekeeper at your hotel (unless you are staying at a B&B that's run by the owners); leave the money each morning before your room is cleaned.

📍 Visitor Information

There are several separate tourism offices in the Florida Keys, and you can use Visit Florida's website (⊕ www.visitflorida.com) for general information and referrals to local agencies.

📅 When to Go

Low Season: Low season is July through October, though holidays and festivals can cause rates to rise to high-season

Essentials

levels. The summer months tend to be the cheapest time to visit, when daily downpours, high humidity, and temperatures in the 90s turn off many visitors.

Shoulder Season: From April through June, winter crowds taper off, hotel rates become reasonable, and the weather is remarkably pleasant, with highs in the 80s and less rain than in the deep summer months.

High Season: Peak season is generally from November through mid-April, when temps are cooler and "snowbirds," or visitors from northern states, fly down to escape cold weather.

WEATHER

From June through September, 90% humidity levels are not uncommon. Thankfully, the weather in the Keys is more moderate than in mainland Florida. Temperatures can be 10°F cooler during the summer and up to 10°F warmer during the winter. The Keys also get substantially less rain than mainland Florida, mostly in quick downpours on summer afternoons. In hurricane season, June through November, the Keys get their fair share of warnings; pay heed, and evacuate earlier rather than later, when flights and automobile traffic get backed up.

What to Pack

CASUAL CLOTHING
Dress is relaxed throughout the Keys—sundresses, sandals, and shorts are appropriate. Clothes should be breathable or, better yet, made of fabric that will drip-dry, since it will be hot and humid.

"RESORT CHIC" OUTFITS
A very small number of restaurants request that men wear jackets and ties but most don't. Where there are dress codes, they tend to be fully adhered to. The strictest places are golf and tennis clubs.

A LIGHT JACKET
Even in summer, ocean breezes can be cool, so bring a lightweight sweater or jacket, and be prepared for air-conditioning in overdrive anywhere.

PRACTICAL SHOES
You'll need your flip-flops for the beach, but also pack a pair of comfortable walking shoes, especially if you plan on doing walking tours in Key West.

SUN PROTECTION
Sunglasses, a hat, and sunscreen are essential for protecting yourself against Florida's strong sun and UV rays, even in overcast conditions. Consider waterproof sunscreens with an SPF of 15 or higher for the most protection. And to protect marine life and coral reefs, choose one without harmful chemicals such as oxybenzone and octinoxate.

A BEACH BAG
There's nothing worse than a car ride in a wet bathing suit. Avoid it by packing a beach bag with underwear and a casual outfit (shorts or a sundress) that's easy to change into. Don't forget a plastic bag for your wet bathing suit.

RAIN GEAR
Be prepared for sudden storms in summer, and note that plastic raincoats are uncomfortable in the high humidity. Often, storms are quick, generally in the afternoon, and the sun comes back in no time.

INSECT REPELLENT
Mosquitoes are always present in Florida, but especially so in the wet summer months. Pack a DEET-based bug spray for the most effective protection.

PORTABLE SPEAKER
The perfect addition to your beach time? Music. Pack waterproof speakers that sync to your phone via Bluetooth.

WATERPROOF PHONE CASE
Whether you want to snap photos while snorkeling or simply protect your device from kids splashing by the pool, pack a waterproof phone case to protect your electronics.

Great Itineraries

IF YOU HAVE 3 DAYS

Spend your first morning diving or snorkeling at John Pennekamp Coral Reef State Park in **Key Largo.** Celebrate sunset with dinner at a waterside restaurant. On Day 2, savor the views on the two-hour drive to Key West. Along the way, stop at Crane Point Museum, Nature Center, and Historic Site in **Marathon.** Another worthwhile detour is Bahia Honda Key State Park on **Bahia Honda Key,** where you can stretch your legs on a nature trail or snorkel on an offshore reef. Once you arrive in **Key West,** watch the sunset at the Mallory Square celebration. The next day, take a trolley tour of Old Town, stroll Duval Street and visit a museum or two, or spend some beach time at Fort Zachary Taylor Historic State Park.

IF YOU HAVE 7 DAYS

Spend your first day as in the three-day itinerary, but stay both the second and third nights in **Islamorada,** fitting in some fishing, boating, or kayaking excursions from Robbie's Marina and a visit to Theater of the Sea. On the fourth morning, head to **Marathon.** Visit Crane Point Museum, Nature Center, and Historic Site and walk out on the Old Seven Mile Bridge or take the ferry to Pigeon Key. Spend the night and head the next morning to Bahia Honda State Park on **Bahia Honda Key** for snorkeling, kayaking, fishing, hiking, and beaching. Spend the night in a waterfront cabin or in the campground. On your sixth day, continue to **Key West,** and get in a little sightseeing before watching the sun set at Mallory Square. Spend the night and your last day visiting the sights, shops, restaurants, and bars in one of America's most lauded vacation spots.

IF YOU HAVE 10 DAYS

To the seven-day itinerary add a few hours on Sombrero Beach in **Marathon** on Day 4, and spend the night in a local resort. Devote Day 6 to snorkeling or diving at Looe Key Reef and a visit to the National Key Deer Refuge on **Big Pine Key.** Spend the night in the Lower Keys before heading to **Key West.** On Day 7, take a break from driving at Fort Zachary Taylor Historic State Park beach. Explore the fort and nearby Eco-Discovery Center. Book ferry passage to **Dry Tortugas National Park** for Day 8 to explore the fort and snorkel in the water surrounding it. Spend the remaining couple of nights and days sampling Key West's attractions and nightlife.

Best Tours

CAPTAIN PIP'S TOURS

The friendly crew at this water-sports hideaway can organize everything from snorkeling trips to the Sombrero Reef (one of the world's largest barrier reefs) to Jet Ski tours and sunset cruises. ⊕ www.captainpips.com

FLORIDA HUMANITIES AUDIO TOURS

Download the free Florida Stories app to take self-guided tours of Islamorada, Indian Key, Key West, and other places. ⊕ floridahumanities.org

FLORIDA KEYS FOOD TOUR

Focusing on dining options in Islamorada, this tour also delves into history and culture by visiting with local artists and taking in sights from the Netflix series *Bloodline*. ⊕ www.flkeysfoodtours.com

KEY LARGO BIKE AND ADVENTURE TOURS

A biking outfit offering everything from two-day bike excursions to three-hour bike tours of Islamorada and the various keys, this tour company will satisfy your two-wheeled ambitions. ⊕ keylargobike.com

KEY LIME BIKE TOUR

The Little White House, the Southernmost Point, Hemingway's house, and the beginning of U.S. Highway 1 are among the stops on this non-strenuous Key West bike tour. Water, helmets, and a slice of key lime pie are included. ⊕ www.keylimebiketours.com

KEYS HELICOPTER TOURS

The pilots at this Marathon-based company provide bird's-eye views of sights like Pigeon Key, Boot Key Harbor, Sombrero Beach, the Seven Mile Bridge, and Bahia Honda State Park. ⊕ www.keyshelicoptertours.com

KEY WEST EXTREME ADVENTURES SHARK TOURS

Fans of *Sharknado* will delight in this two-hour marine-life tour aboard a 34-foot catamaran that also includes sightings of dolphins, sea turtles, and stingrays. ⊕ www.keywestextremeadventures.com

KEY WEST FOOD TOURS

Wear comfy shoes (and loose-fitting pants!) for these three-hour tasting odysseys. Popular options include the seafood-focused tour and the Cuban- and Caribbean-influenced Southernmost Food and Culture Tour. ⊕ www.keywestfoodtours.com

Best Tours

KEY WEST GHOST AND MYSTERIES TOUR

Knowledgeable guides help you glimpse the haunted and hidden side of Key West on this 90-minute walking tour. ⊕ key-westghostandmysteriestour.com

KEY WEST PUB CRAWL

This 2½-hour tour stops at five bars and includes cocktails and a T-shirt. Contests, trivia, and comedy make this a popular nightlife excursion. ⊕ keywest-walkingtours.com/pub-crawls

On the Calendar

January

Florida Keys Seafood Festival. Local seafood, chef demonstrations, and live music mark this event ⊕ www.floridakeysseafoodfestival.com.

Key West Food & Wine Festival. More than 30 unique events make up this festival, including waterfront tastings and winemaker and chef collaborations. ⊕ keywestfoodandwinefestival.com.

March

Original Marathon Seafood Festival. Held annually since the 1970s, this two-day seafood bacchanalia features live music as well as 200 vendors selling crafts, jewelry, and art. ⊕ marathonseafoodfestival.com.

April

Conch Republic Independence Celebration. This 10-day event honors Key West's eccentric community with races and parties. ⊕ conchrepublic.com.

June

Big Pine and Lower Keys Dolphin Tournament. Mahimahi is the catch; so is more than $35,000 in prize money. ⊕ fish-florida.com.

July

Hemingway Days. One of Key West's most popular events includes a highly competitive Hemingway look-alike contest, poetry readings, and a marlin tournament. ⊕ fla-keys.com/hemingway-days.

August

Lobsterfest. To celebrate lobster season, Key West throws this annual event featuring the tasty crustacean, as well as free concerts and other entertainment. ⊕ keywestlobsterfest.com.

October

Fantasy Fest. Thousands of people—often in outrageous costumes—attend this week-long Key West street party. ⊕ www.fantasyfest.com.

December

Islamorada Sailfish Tournament. The competition calendar in the so-called Sport-Fishing Capital of the World starts with this event. ⊕ www.islamorada-sailfishtournament.com.

Contacts

Air

AIRLINE CONTACTS American Airlines. ✉ 3491 S Roosevelt Blvd., Key West ☎ 800/433–7300 ⊕ www.aa.com. **Delta.** ✉ 3491 S Roosevelt Blvd., Key West ☎ 800/221–1212 for U.S. reservations, 800/241–4141 for international reservations ⊕ www.delta.com. **Silver Airways.** ✉ 3491 S Roosevelt Blvd., Key West ☎ 801/401–9100 reservations ⊕ www.silverairways.com. **United.** ✉ 3491 S Roosevelt Blvd., Key West ☎ 800/864–8331 for U.S. reservations, 800/538–2929 for international reservations ⊕ www.united.com.

AIRPORT CONTACTS Fort Lauderdale–Hollywood International Airport (FLL). ✉ 100 Terminal Dr., Fort Lauderdale ☎ 866/435–9355 ⊕ www.broward.org/airport. **Key West International Airport (EYW).** ✉ 3491 S. Roosevelt Blvd., Key West ☎ 305/809–5200 ⊕ eyw.com. **Miami International Airport (MIA).** ✉ 2100 NW 42nd Ave., Miami ☎ 305/876–7000, 800/825–5642 international ⊕ www.iflymia.com.

SHUTTLE CONTACTS Greyhound. ✉ 3439 S Roosevelt Blvd., Key West ☎ 800/231–2222 ⊕ www.greyhound.com. **Keys Shuttle.** ✉ 1333 Overseas Hwy., Marathon ☎ 888/765–9997 ⊕ www.keysshuttle.com.

Boat and Ferry

CONTACTS Key West Express. ✉ 100 Grinnell St., Key West ☎ 239/463–5733 ⊕ www.keywestexpress.net.

Bus

CONTACTS City of Key West Department of Transportation. ✉ 5701 College Rd., Key West ☎ 305/809–3910 ⊕ www.kwtransit.com.

Car

CAR CONTACTS Florida's Turnpike Enterprise. ☎ 800/749–7453 ⊕ www.floridasturnpike.com. **SunPass.** ☎ 888/865–5352 ⊕ www.sunpass.com.

CAR RENTAL CONTACTS Avis. ✉ Key West ☎ 800/352–7900 ⊕ www.avis.com. **Budget.** ✉ Key West ☎ 800/214–6094 ⊕ www.budget.com. **Hertz.** ✉ Key West ☎ 800/654–3131 ⊕ www.hertz.com.

Taxi

CONTACTS Key Lime Transport. ✉ Key West ☎ 305/539-0575 ⊕ www.keylimetransportation.com.

Chapter 3

THE UPPER KEYS

Updated by
Sara Liss

⊙ Sights	🍴 Restaurants	🛏 Hotels	🛍 Shopping	🍸 Nightlife
★★★★☆	★★★★☆	★★★★☆	★★★☆☆	★★★☆☆

WELCOME TO THE UPPER KEYS

TOP REASONS TO GO

★ **Snorkeling:** The best snorkeling spots in these parts are found around the awe-inspiring *Christ of the Deep,* east of John Pennekamp Coral Reef State Park in the Florida Keys National Marine Sanctuary.

★ **Sunsets:** Find a comfortable place to watch the sunset, keeping an eye out for the elusive green flash.

★ **Aquatic mammals:** Get up close and personal with sea life at Theater of the Sea.

★ **Boating:** Start with a visit to Robbie's Marina on Lower Matecumbe Key in Islamorada, a salty spot to find everything from fishing charters to kayak rentals.

★ **Nightlife:** It's not a disco, but you can dance the night away to music by local bands at The Lorelei's Cabana Bar.

1 Key Largo. Thirty-mile-long Key Largo is the largest island in the chain and is considered the gateway to the Keys. Expect plenty of water sports, especially snorkeling and diving, fresh seafood at casual waterfront restaurants and bars, and glorious sunsets.

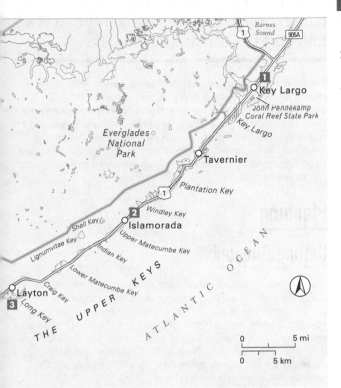

2 Islamorada. Islamorada (pronounced *eye*-la-more- *ah*-da) is known as the "sport fishing capital of the world," and numerous fishing tournaments take place here. Charters can be arranged at local marinas. It is also home to several nature-rich state parks.

3 Long Key. Long Key is decidedly low-key and attracts nature lovers, hikers, campers, anglers, and those looking to de-stress. Dominated by Long Key State Park, visitors can hike on trails amid mangroves and canoe along lagoons. There's also a beach that's popular with snorkelers.

Diving and snorkeling rule in the Upper Keys, thanks to North America's only living coral barrier reef, which runs a few miles off the Atlantic coast.

Fishing is another huge draw, especially around Islamorada, known for its sport fishing. But true nature lovers won't feel shortchanged. Within 1½ miles of the bay coast lie the mangrove trees and sandy shores of Everglades National Park, where you'll see endangered manatees, curious dolphins, and other marine creatures. Bird watchers will find plenty to see, including the rare Everglades snail kites, bald eagles, ospreys, and a colorful array of egrets and herons.

Planning

Getting Oriented

The best way to explore this stretch, or any stretch, of the Florida Keys is by boat. As soon as possible you should jump on any sea-worthy vessel to see the view of and from the water. And make sure you veer off the main drag of U.S. 1. Head toward the water, where you'll often find the kind of laid-back restaurants and hotels that define the Keys. John Pennekamp Coral Reef State Park is the region's most popular destination, but it's certainly not the only place to get in touch with nature.

Getting Here and Around

Greyhound (about $25 per person), Keys Transportation ($49 per person), and Keys Shuttle (about $70 per person) all offer shared-ride transportation to the Keys with various stops. SuperShuttle charges about $280 for up to 10 passengers for nonstop trips from Miami International Airport to the Upper Keys. Shared-ride trips are also available. For trips to the airport, place your request 24 hours in advance.

Hotels

Most lodgings are in small, narrow, waterfront complexes with efficiencies and one- or two-bedroom units. These places offer dockage and often arrange boating, diving, and fishing excursions. There are also full-scale resorts with every type of activity imaginable and smaller boutique hotels where the attraction is personalized service.

Restaurants

The Upper Keys are full of low-key eateries, where the owner is also the chef and the food is tasty and never too fussy. The one exception is Islamorada, where you'll find more upscale restaurants, but Key Largo has a few that can compete plate for plate. Restaurants may close for a two- to four-week vacation during the slow season between early September and mid-November.

Hotel and restaurant reviews have been shortened. For full information, visit Fodors.com. Hotel prices are the lowest cost of a standard double room in high season. Restaurant prices are the average cost of a main course at dinner or, if dinner is not served, at lunch.

What It Costs			
$	$$	$$$	$$$$
RESTAURANTS			
under $20	$20–$25	$26–$35	over $35
HOTELS			
under $200	$200–$300	$301–$400	over $400

Key Largo

56 miles south of Miami International Airport (between MM 107 and 91).

The first of the Upper Keys reachable by car, 30-mile-long Key Largo is the largest island in the chain. Key Largo—named Cayo Largo (Long Key) by the Spanish—makes a great introduction to the region. This is the gateway to the Keys, and an evening of fresh seafood and views of the sunset on the water will get you in the right state of mind.

The history of Largo reads much like that of the rest of the Keys: a succession of native people, pirates, wreckers, and developers. The first settlement on Key Largo was named Planter, back in the days of pineapple and, later, key lime plantations. For a time it was a convenient shipping port, but when the railroad arrived Planter died on the vine. Today, three communities—North Key Largo, Key Largo, and the separately incorporated city of Tavernier—make up the whole of Key Largo.

GETTING HERE AND AROUND

Key Largo is 56 miles south of Miami International Airport, with its mile markers ranging from 106 to 91. The island runs northeast–southwest, with the Overseas Highway (U.S. 1), divided by a median most of the way, running down the center. If the highway is your only glimpse of the island, you're likely to feel barraged by its tacky commercial side. Make a point of driving Route 905 in North Key Largo and down side streets to get a better feel for it.

VISITOR INFORMATION

Stop by the Key Largo Chamber of Commerce for information or some colorful gifts (it sells a surprising selection of women's clothing). Divers take note: the Florida Keys National Marine Sanctuary has an office in Key Largo.

CONTACTS Florida Keys National Marine Sanctuary. ⊠ MM 95.23 BS, 95230 Overseas Hwy, Key Largo ☎ 305/852–7717 ⊕ floridakeys.noaa.gov. **Key Largo Chamber of Commerce.** ⊠ MM 106 BS, 10600 Overseas Hwy., Key Largo ☎ 305/451–4747, 800/822–1088 ⊕ www.keylargochamber.org.

Sights

Dagny Johnson Key Largo Hammock Botanical State Park

OTHER ATTRACTION | FAMILY | American crocodiles, mangrove cuckoos, white-crowned pigeons, mahogany mistletoe, wild cotton, and 100 other rare critters and plants inhabit these 2,400 acres, between Crocodile Lake National Wildlife Refuge and the waters of Pennekamp Coral Reef State Park. The park is also a user-friendly place to explore the largest remaining stand of the vast West Indian tropical hardwood hammock and mangrove wetland that once covered most of the Keys. ⊠ Rte. 905 OS, North Key Largo ✛ ½ mile north of Overseas Hwy. ☎ 305/451–1202 ⊕ www.floridastateparks.org/parks-and-trails/dagny-johnson-key-largo-hammock-botanical-state-park ☞ $3 (exact change needed for the honor box).

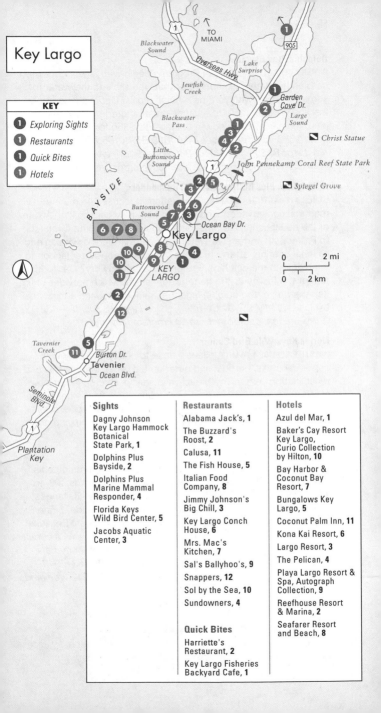

Key Largo

KEY

- **1** Exploring Sights
- **1** Restaurants
- **1** Quick Bites
- **1** Hotels

TO MIAMI

Blackwater Sound

Overseas Hwy.

Lake Surprise

Jewfish Creek

Garden Cove Dr.

Blackwater Pass

Large Sound

Christ Statue

Little Buttonwood Sound

John Pennekamp Coral Reef State Park

Spiegel Grove

BAYSIDE

Buttonwood Sound

Ocean Bay Dr.

Key Largo

KEY LARGO

0   2 mi

0   2 km

Tavernier Creek

Burton Dr.

Tavenier

Ocean Blvd.

Seminole Blvd.

Plantation Key

Sights

Dagny Johnson Key Largo Hammock Botanical State Park, **1**

Dolphins Plus Bayside, **2**

Dolphins Plus Marine Mammal Responder, **4**

Florida Keys Wild Bird Center, **5**

Jacobs Aquatic Center, **3**

Restaurants

Alabama Jack's, **1**

The Buzzard's Roost, **2**

Calusa, **11**

The Fish House, **5**

Italian Food Company, **8**

Jimmy Johnson's Big Chill, **3**

Key Largo Conch House, **6**

Mrs. Mac's Kitchen, **7**

Sal's Ballyhoo's, **9**

Snappers, **12**

Sol by the Sea, **10**

Sundowners, **4**

Quick Bites

Harriette's Restaurant, **2**

Key Largo Fisheries Backyard Cafe, **1**

Hotels

Azul del Mar, **1**

Baker's Cay Resort Key Largo, Curio Collection by Hilton, **10**

Bay Harbor & Coconut Bay Resort, **7**

Bungalows Key Largo, **5**

Coconut Palm Inn, **11**

Kona Kai Resort, **6**

Largo Resort, **3**

The Pelican, **4**

Playa Largo Resort & Spa, Autograph Collection, **9**

Reefhouse Resort & Marina, **2**

Seafarer Resort and Beach, **8**

Dolphins Plus Bayside

OTHER ATTRACTION | FAMILY | Programs begin with a get-acquainted session beneath a tiki hut. After that, you slip into the water for some frolicking with your new dolphin pals. Options range from a shallow-water swim to a hands-on structured swim with a dolphin. You can also shadow a trainer—it's $350 for a half day or a hefty $630 for a full day. ⊠ *MM 101.9 BS, 101900 Overseas Hwy., Key Largo* ☎ *305/451–4060, 866/860–7946* ⊕ *www.dolphinsplus. com* ⊠ *Admission only $20, interactive programs from $59.*

★ Dolphins Plus Marine Mammal Responder

OTHER ATTRACTION | FAMILY | This nonprofit focuses on marine mammal conservation, and you can help it by participating in one of the educational offerings. One popular option is the Connect to Protect, an immersive water program that begins with an educational briefing, after which you enter the deep-water lagoon to interact with the dolphins. Prefer to stay mostly dry? Opt for the tour of the facility or the general admission, which provides unlimited viewing of the dolphin lagoons, trainer talks, and educational exhibits. ⊠ *MM 99, 31 Corrine Pl., Key Largo* ☎ *305/453–4321* ⊕ *www.connecttoprotect.org* ⊠ *Programs from $59.*

Florida Keys Wild Bird Center

WILDLIFE REFUGE | FAMILY | Have a nose-to-beak encounter with ospreys, hawks, herons, and other unreleasable birds at this bird rehabilitation center. The birds live in spacious screened enclosures along a boardwalk running through some of the best waterfront real estate in the Keys. ⊠ *MM 93.6 BS, 93600 Overseas Hwy., Key Largo* ☎ *305/852–4486* ⊕ *www.keepthemflying.org* ⊠ *Free, donations accepted.*

Jacobs Aquatic Center

POOL | FAMILY | Take the plunge at one of three swimming pools: an eight-lane, 25-meter lap pool with two diving boards; a 3- to 4-foot-deep pool accessible to people with mobility challenges; and an interactive children's play pool with a waterslide, pirate ship, waterfall, and sloping zero-entry instead of steps. Because so few of the motels in Key Largo have pools, it remains a popular destination for visiting families. ⊠ *Key Largo Community Park, 320 Laguna Ave., at St. Croix Pl., Key Largo* ☎ *305/453–7946* ⊕ *www.jacobsaquaticcenter.org* ⊠ *$10 weekdays, $12 weekends.*

 Beaches

★ John Pennekamp Coral Reef State Park

BEACH | FAMILY | This state park is on everyone's list for easy access to the best diving and snorkeling in Florida. The underwater

A beautiful underwater scene at John Pennekamp Coral Reef State Park on Key Largo

treasure encompasses 78 nautical square miles of coral reefs and sea-grass beds. It lies adjacent to the Florida Keys National Marine Sanctuary, which contains 40 of the 52 species of coral in the Atlantic Reef System and nearly 600 varieties of fish, from the colorful parrotfish to the demure cocoa damselfish. Whatever you do, get in the water. Snorkeling and diving trips ($39 and $90, respectively; equipment extra) and glass-bottom-boat rides to the reef ($32) are available, weather permitting. One of the most popular snorkel trips is to see *Christ of the Deep,* the 2-ton underwater statue of Jesus. The park also has nature trails, two manmade beaches, picnic shelters, a snack bar, and a campground. **Amenities:** food and drink; parking (fee); showers; toilets; water sports. **Best for:** snorkeling; swimming. ⊠ *MM 102.5 OS, 102601 Overseas Hwy., Key Largo* ☎ *305/451–1202 for park, 305/451–6300 for excursions* ⊕ *pennekamppark.com* ⌦ *$4 for 1 person in vehicle, $8 for 2–8 people, $2 for pedestrians and cyclists or extra people (plus a 50¢ per-person county surcharge).*

🍴 Restaurants

Alabama Jack's

$ | **SEAFOOD** | Calories be damned—the conch fritters here are heaven on a plate. Come early for dinner (Jack's closes by 6:30, when the mosquitos start biting), and come hungry; the free-form fritters are large and loaded with flavor. **Known for:** heavenly conch fritters; unique setting (about a 30-minute drive from Key Largo);

live music. $ *Average main: $11* ⊠ *58000 Card Sound Rd., Key Largo* ☎ *305/248–8741* ⊕ *www.facebook.com/realalabamajacks.*

★ The Buzzard's Roost

$$ | SEAFOOD | The views are nice at this waterfront restaurant, but the food is what gets your attention. Burgers, fish tacos, and seafood baskets are lunch faves. **Known for:** marina views; daily chef's specials; Sunday brunch with live steel drums. $ *Average main: $21* ⊠ *Garden Cove Marina, 21 Garden Cove Dr., Key Largo* ☎ *305/453–3746* ⊕ *www.buzzardsroostkeylargo.com.*

★ Calusa

$$$ | CARIBBEAN | Nestled on the third floor of the main building of Baker's Cay Resort, this waterfront spot offers panoramic views of the Gulf and a creative menu of Creole-Caribbean-inspired dishes. Start off with a round of craft cocktails (the Dark Rum Sazerac is a popular one), and then head to a table on the multilevel balcony for a dinner of Keys pink shrimp and lobster pasta or local mahimahi with miso-honey glaze. **Known for:** spectacular views; creative cocktails; whole fried fish. $ *Average main: $28* ⊠ *Baker's Cay Resort, MM 97 BS, 97000 Overseas Hwy., 3rd fl., Key Largo* ☎ *305/852–5553* ⊕ *www.bakerscay.com.*

The Fish House

$$ | SEAFOOD | Restaurants not on the water have to produce the highest-quality food to survive in the Keys. Try fish Matecumbe style—baked with tomatoes, capers, olive oil, and lemon juice— or the buttery pan-sautéed preparation. **Known for:** smoked fish chunks and dip; excellent key lime pie; fresh-as-can-be seafood served fast. $ *Average main: $21* ⊠ *MM 102.4 OS, 102341 Overseas Hwy., Key Largo* ☎ *305/451–4665* ⊕ *www.fishhouse.com.*

★ Italian Food Company

$ | ITALIAN | FAMILY | Authentic southern Italian cuisine, with freshly made Neapolitan (Naples-style) pizza, pastas, and desserts is the focus here. A nicely landscaped garden with a cute Fiat decked out in the colors of the Italian flag should alert you to founders Tony and Isis Wright's obsession with detail. **Known for:** friendly service; Neopolitan pizza; a second location in Islamorada. $ *Average main: $17* ⊠ *98070 Overseas Hwy., Key Largo* ☎ *305/440– 2700* ⊕ *italianfoodcompany.com* ⊙ *Closed Tues.*

Jimmy Johnson's Big Chill

$$ | SEAFOOD | Owned by former NFL coach Jimmy Johnson, this waterfront establishment offers three experiences: the best sports bar in the Upper Keys, an all-glass dining room with a waterfront deck, and an enormous outdoor tiki bar with entertainment seven nights a week. There's even a pool and cabanas where (for a fee) you can spend the day sunning. **Known for:** the place to watch a game; fantastic bay views; brick-oven chicken wings with rosemary. $ *Average main: $24 ⊠ MM 104 BS, 104000 Overseas Hwy., Key Largo ☎ 305/453–9066 ⊕ www. jjsbigchill.com.*

Key Largo Conch House

$ | **AMERICAN** | This family-owned restaurant in a Victorian-style home tucked into the trees is worth seeking out. Seven varieties of Benedict, including conch, are brunch favorites, while lunch and dinner menus highlight local seafood like lionfish (when available) and yellowtail snapper. **Known for:** shrimp and grits; all-season outside dining; seafood tacos. $ *Average main: $16 ⊠ MM 100.2, 100211 Overseas Hwy., Key Largo ☎ 305/453–4844 ⊕ www. keylargoconchhouse.com ⊗ Closed Thurs.*

Mrs. Mac's Kitchen

$ | **SEAFOOD | FAMILY** | Locals pack the counters and booths at this tiny eatery, where license plates decorate the walls, to dine on everything from blackened prime rib to crab cakes. Every night is themed, including Meatloaf Monday, Italian Wednesday, and Seafood Sensation (offered Friday and Saturday). **Known for:** a second location a half mile south with a full liquor bar; champagne breakfast; being a stop on the Florida Keys Food Tour. $ *Average main: $17 ⊠ MM 99.4 BS, 99336 Overseas Hwy., Key Largo ☎ 305/451–3722, 305/451–6227 ⊕ www.mrsmacskitchen.com ⊗ Closed Sun.*

Sal's Ballyhoo's

$$ | **SEAFOOD | FAMILY** | Occupying a 1930s conch house with outdoor seating right alongside U.S. 1 under the sea-grape trees, this local favorite is all about the fish: yellowtail snapper, tuna, and mahimahi. Choose your favorite, then choose your preparation, such as the Hemingway, with a Parmesan crust, crabmeat, and key lime butter. **Known for:** spicy corn muffins; fish and fried-tomato sandwich; grilled avocado appetizer. $ *Average main: $24 ⊠ MM 97.8 median, 97800 Overseas Hwy., Key Largo ☎ 305/852–0822 ⊕ www.ballyhoosrestaurant.com.*

Snappers

$$ | **SEAFOOD** | In a lively waterfront setting, Snappers has live music, Sunday brunch (including a build-your-own Bloody Mary bar), killer rum drinks, and seating alongside the fishing dock. The crab cakes are famous, as is the Bahamian cocktail sauce that accompanies them. **Known for:** grouper Oscar style; deep-fried gator bites doused in blue-cheese dressing; happening vibe and a local crowd. $ *Average main: $20 ⊠ MM 94.5 OS, 139 Seaside Ave., Key Largo ☎ 305/852–5956 ⊕ www.snapperskeylargo.com.*

★ Sol by the Sea

$$ | CARIBBEAN | This is the spot you might imagine when you think of dining by the water in the Keys. The Caribbean-influenced menu includes things like lobster and shrimp cakes, fried whole fish (the presentation is a photo op), and catch of the day served with fried plantains and rice and beans. **Known for:** picturesque spot; unique key lime dessert; Caribbean-influenced seafood. $ *Average main: $25* ⊠ *Playa Largo Resort, MM 97 BS, 97540 Overseas Hwy., Key Largo* ☎ *305/853–1001* ⊕ *www.playalargoresort.com.*

Sundowners

$$$ | AMERICAN | If it's a clear night and you can snag a reservation, this restaurant will treat you to a sherbet-hue sunset over Florida Bay. Try the key lime seafood, a happy combo of sautéed shrimp, lobster, and crabmeat swimming in a tangy sauce spiked with Tabasco served over penne or rice. **Known for:** bacon-wrapped scallops; sunset views; choose your fish, choose your preparation. $ *Average main: $29* ⊠ *MM 104 BS, 103900 Overseas Hwy., Key Largo* ☎ *305/451–4502* ⊕ *sundownerskeylargo.com.*

☕ Coffee and Quick Bites

Harriette's Restaurant

$ | AMERICAN | If you're looking for comfort food—like melt-in-your-mouth key lime biscuits the size of a salad plate or old-fashioned hot cakes with sausage or bacon—try this refreshing throwback for a hearty breakfast. At lunch, Harriette's shines in the burger department, and all the soups—from garlic tomato to chili—are homemade. **Known for:** a wait—but worth it; best muffins in Key Largo; tight dining space. $ *Average main: $10* ⊠ *MM 95.7 BS, 95710 Overseas Hwy., Key Largo* ☎ *305/852–8689* ⊕ *www. harriettesrestaurant.com* ⊗ *No dinner* ⌇ *American Express not accepted.*

Key Largo Fisheries Backyard Cafe

$ | AMERICAN | This waterfront café serves locally sourced seafood, soups, and salads in a casual setting—specifically, the back of Key Largo Fisheries. Order at the counter, find a picnic table on the covered patio, and watch the boats come in as your food is prepared. **Known for:** fresh seafood; easy to-go ordering; happy hour. $ *Average main: $16* ⊠ *1313 Ocean Bay Dr., Ste. A, Key Largo* ☎ *305/451–3784* ⊕ *www.keylargofisheries.com/cafe.*

Hotels

Azul del Mar

$$ | B&B/INN | The dock points the way to beautiful sunsets at this adults-only boutique hotel, which has been transformed from a run-down mom-and-pop place into a waterfront gem. **Pros:** high-quality linens; good location; sophisticated design. **Cons:** small beach; could use a refresh; minimum stays during holidays. ⑤ *Rooms from: $299 ⊠ MM 104.3 BS, 104300 Overseas Hwy., Key Largo ☎ 305/451–0337, 008/263–2985 ⊕ www.azulkeylargo. com ⇄ 6 units* ⑩ *No Meals.*

★ Baker's Cay Resort Key Largo, Curio Collection by Hilton

$$$ | RESORT | FAMILY | Nestled within a "hardwood hammock" (localese for uplands habitat where hardwood trees such as live oak grow) near the southern border of Everglades National Park, this sprawling, 13-acre resort is not to be missed. **Pros:** you never have to leave the resort; pretty pools with waterfalls; 21-slip marina for all your boating needs. **Cons:** some rooms overlook the parking lot; pools are near the highway; high per-night resort fee. ⑤ *Rooms from: $399 ⊠ MM 97 BS, 97000 Overseas Hwy., Key Largo ☎ 305/852–5553, 888/871–3437 ⊕ www.keylargoresort. com ⇄ 200 rooms* ⑩ *No Meals.*

Bay Harbor & Coconut Bay Resort

$ | RESORT | FAMILY | Some 200 feet of waterfront is the main attraction at these side-by-side sister properties that offer a choice between smaller rooms and larger freestanding cottages. **Pros:** temperature-controlled pool; owner Peg's amazing homemade scones; free use of kayaks, paddleboats, and paddleboards. **Cons:** a bit dated; small sea-walled sand beach; bring your own charcoal for the barbecue grills. ⑤ *Rooms from: $195 ⊠ MM 97.7 BS, 97702 Overseas Hwy., Key Largo ☎ 305/852–1625, 800/385–0986 ⊕ www.bayharborkeylargo.com ⇄ 21 units* ⑩ *Free Breakfast.*

★ Bungalows Key Largo

$$$$ | ALL-INCLUSIVE | This 12-acre, adults-only hideaway has charming freestanding bungalows (some of which are waterfront) that are outfitted with a front porch with Adirondack chairs, a sitting area with a couch, and a private patio with an outdoor soaking tub, shower, and seating area. **Pros:** only all-inclusive resort in the Keys; relaxing atmosphere; a lavish spa. **Cons:** gratuities are charged separately; two-night minimum stay; extra fees for early arrival and late checkout. ⑤ *Rooms from: $990 ⊠ MM 99, 99010 Overseas Hwy., Key Largo ☎ 305/363–2830 ⊕ bungalowskeylargo.com ⇄ 135 suites* ⑩ *All-Inclusive.*

Coconut Palm Inn

$$ | B&B/INN | FAMILY | This waterfront haven is tucked into a residential neighborhood beneath towering palms and native gumbo-limbos. **Pros:** secluded and quiet; 100% smoke-free resort; sophisticated feel. **Cons:** front desk closes early each evening; no access to ice machine when staff leave; no dining on site. $ *Rooms from: $299* ✉ *MM 92 BS, 198 Harborview Dr., via Jo-Jean Way off Overseas Hwy., Key Largo* ☎ *305/852–3017* ⊕ *www.coconutpalminn.com* ⤴ *20 rooms* ¶⃝ *Free Breakfast.*

★ Kona Kai Resort

$$ | RESORT | Brilliantly colored bougainvillea, coconut palm, and guava trees—and a botanical garden of other rare species—make this 2-acre adult hideaway one of the prettiest places to stay in the Keys. **Pros:** friendly staff; free use of sports equipment; spa-like pool area. **Cons:** expensive; some rooms are very close together; no restaurant on site. $ *Rooms from: $299* ✉ *MM 97.8 BS, 97802 Overseas Hwy., Key Largo* ☎ *305/852–7200, 800/365–7829* ⊕ *www.konakairesort.com* ⤴ *13 rooms* ¶⃝ *Free Breakfast.*

Largo Resort

$$$$ | RESORT | Behind 10-foot, dark-wood Kong gates is a Bali-inspired world, where tranquility washes over you like a rain shower. **Pros:** unrivaled privacy; free kayaks and paddleboards; weekday special rates. **Cons:** no food or drinks on site for purchase; removed from sights; quietude isn't for everyone. $ *Rooms from: $500* ✉ *MM 101.7 BS, 101740 Overseas Hwy., Key Largo* ☎ *305/451–0424* ⊕ *www.largoresort.com* ⤴ *6 bungalows* ¶⃝ *No Meals.*

The Pelican

$ | HOTEL | FAMILY | This 1950s throwback recalls the days when parents packed the kids into the station wagon and headed to no-frills seaside motels. **Pros:** free use of kayaks and a canoe; well-maintained dock; reasonable rates. **Cons:** some rooms are small; basic accommodations and amenities; road noise with some units. $ *Rooms from: $159* ✉ *MM 99.3, 99340 Overseas Hwy., Key Largo* ☎ *305/451–3576, 877/451–3576* ⊕ *www.pelican-keylargo.com* ⤴ *32 units* ¶⃝ *Free Breakfast.*

★ Playa Largo Resort & Spa, Autograph Collection

$$$ | RESORT | FAMILY | At this luxurious, 14-acre, bayfront retreat, you'll find one of the nicest beaches in the Keys, as well as water sports galore, bocce, tennis, basketball, and a fitness center with inspiring pool views. **Pros:** comfortable rooms, most with balconies; large pool; nightly sunset celebration. **Cons:** hefty resort fee; pool can get crowded; luxury will cost you. $ *Rooms from: $399*

⊠ *MM 97.4, 97450 Overseas Hwy., Key Largo* ☎ *305/853–1001*
⊕ *playalargoresort.com* ⇱ *178 units* ⦿ *No Meals.*

Reefhouse Resort & Marina

$$$ | **RESORT** | **FAMILY** | Set on 17 acres overlooking Blackwater
Sound, this hotel has been given a much-needed refresh, including the rooms, which span traditional and two-bedroom suite-style
accommodations. **Pros:** lots of activities; dive shop on property;
free Wi-Fi. **Cons:** rooms facing highway can be noisy; thin walls;
chain-hotel feel. ⑤ *Rooms from: $359* ⊠ *MM 103.8 BS, 103800
Overseas Hwy., Key Largo* ☎ *305/453–0000, 866/849–3753*
⊕ *www.opalcollection.com/reefhouse* ⇱ *153 rooms* ⦿ *No Meals.*

Seafarer Resort and Beach

$ | **HOTEL** | **FAMILY** | At this basic, budget lodging it's all about stay-
ing on the water for a song. **Pros:** kitchen units available; complimentary kayak use; cheap rates. **Cons:** can hear road noise in
some rooms; some complaints about cleanliness; decor could use
an upgrade. ⑤ *Rooms from: $149* ⊠ *MM 97.6 BS, 97684 Overseas
Hwy., Key Largo* ☎ *305/852–5349* ⊕ *www.seafarerkeylargo.com*
⇱ *15 units* ⦿ *Free Breakfast.*

Nightlife

Breezer's Tiki Bar

BARS | Mingle with locals over cocktails and catch amazing sun-
sets from the comfort of an enclosed, air-conditioned bar. Floor-to-
ceiling doors can be opened on cool days and closed on hot days.
⊠ *Reefhouse Resort & Marina, MM 103.8 BS, 103800 Overseas
Hwy., Key Largo* ☎ *305/453–0000.*

★ C&C Wood Fired Eats

WINE BARS | Although it's only open till 10, this is still a place to
see and be seen. It's dark and a little mysterious, and the wine,
wood-fired pizzas, cheese pairings, meats, and fondues are
five-star worthy. Sit at the bar, on a couch, or at a high-top, and
be transported to somewhere other than a typical, tropical Keys
venue. The daily happy hour offers a "pizza and pitcher" special
that's a hit with locals. ⊠ *MM 9.2, 99201 Overseas Hwy., Key
Largo* ☎ *305/451–0995* ⊕ *candcwoodfiredeats.com.*

Caribbean Club

BARS | Walls plastered with Bogart memorabilia remind customers
that the classic 1948 Bogart-Bacall flick *Key Largo* has a connection with this watering hole. Although no food is served, and the
floors are bare concrete, this landmark draws boaters, curious
visitors, and local barflies to its humble barstools and pool tables.
But the real magic is around back, where you can grab a seat on

the deck and catch a postcard-perfect sunset. Live music draws revelers Thursday through Sunday. ⌧ *MM 104 BS, 104080 Overseas Hwy., Key Largo* ☎ *305/451–4466* ⊕ *caribbeanclubkl.com.*

Skipper's Dockside

CAFÉS | FAMILY | Marina views are among the many charms of this fun place in the heart of Key Largo. Sit outside under the tiki, in a brightly colored Adirondack chair by the firepits, or inside amid driftwood walls and prize catches. No matter: what you'll remember is the fresh, everything-made-in-house food. ⌧ *MM 100 OS, 528 Caribbean Dr., Key Largo* ☎ *305/453–9794* ⊕ *www. skippersdockside.com.*

Shopping

Key Lime Products

OTHER SPECIALTY STORE | Go into olfactory overload—you'll find yourself sniffing every single bar of soap and scented candle inside this key lime treasure trove. Take home some key lime juice (super-easy pie-making directions are right on the bottle), marmalade, candies, sauces, and even key lime shampoo. ⌧ *MM 95.2 BS, 95231 Overseas Hwy., Key Largo* ☎ *305/853–0378, 800/870–1780* ⊕ *www.keylimeproducts.com.*

★ Keys Chocolates & Ice Cream

CHOCOLATE | FAMILY | The only chocolate factory in the Keys specializes in key lime truffles. In addition to fine white, milk, and dark Belgian-chocolate confections (the salted turtles, a fan favorite, are worth every calorie), you'll find cupcakes and ice cream. Chocolate-making classes are also available for kids and adults, and a small gift area showcases local art, jewelry, hot sauces, and other goodies. ⌧ *MM 100 BS, 100471 Overseas Hwy., Key Largo* ☎ *305/453–6613* ⊕ *www.keylargochocolates.com.*

★ Old Road Gallery

ART GALLERIES | This shop is filled with ceramics, bronze and copper creations, and jewelry—all made by local artists—but it's the secret sculpture garden that really makes this place unique. Further, owner-artists Cindy and Dwayne King genuinely embody the joyful spirit of the Florida Keys. ⌧ *88888 Old Hwy., Tavernier* ✛ *In the median between Overseas Hwy. and Old Hwy.* ☎ *305/852–8935* ⊕ *www.oldroadgallery.com.*

Randy's Florida Keys Gift Company

SOUVENIRS | Since 1989, this has been *the* place for unique gifts for every budget. Owner Randy and his wife, Lisa, aren't only fantastic at stocking the store with a plethora of items, but they're also well respected in the community for their generosity and dedication. ⊠ *MM 102.5, 102421 Overseas Hwy., Key Largo* ✛ *On U.S. 1, next to the Sandal Factory Outlet* ☎ *305/453–9229* ⊕ *www.keysmermaid.com.*

Shell World

SOUVENIRS | Lots of shops in the Keys sell cheesy souvenirs—snow globes, alligator hats, shell-encrusted anything—and this is the granddaddy of them all. But at this sprawling building in the median of the Overseas Highway, you'll also find high-end clothing, jewelry, housewares, artwork, and keepsakes that range from delightfully tacky to tasteful. ⊠ *MM 97.5, 97600 Overseas Hwy., Key Largo* ☎ *305/852–8245, 888/398–6233* ⊕ *www.shellworld-flkeys.com.*

Activities

BIKING
Bubba's

BIKING | Bubba's organizes one-week custom biking tours through the Keys along the Heritage Trail. A van accompanies tours to carry luggage and tired riders. Former police officer Bubba Barron also hosts a weeklong ride down the length of the Keys every November. Riders can opt for tent camping or motel-room accommodations. Meals are included, but bike rentals are extra. ⊠ *Key Largo* ☎ *321/759–3433* ⊕ *www.bubbaspamperedpedalers.com* ⊠ *From $1,210 per person, double occupancy.*

BOATING
Everglades Eco-Tours

BOATING | FAMILY | For more than 30 years, Captain Sterling has operated Everglades and Florida Bay ecology tours and sunset cruises. With his expert guidance, you can see dolphins, manatees, and birds from a pontoon boat equipped with PVC chairs. Bring your own food and drinks; each tour has a maximum of six people. ⊠ *Sundowners Restaurant, MM 104 BS, 103900 Overseas Hwy., Key Largo* ☎ *305/853–5161, 888/224–6044* ⊕ *www.captainsterling.com* ⊠ *From $59.*

M. V. Key Largo Princess

BOATING | FAMILY | Two-hour glass-bottom-boat trips and pricier sunset cruises on a 70-foot motor yacht with a large glass viewing area depart from the Holiday Inn docks three times a day. ■**TIP**➜ **Purchase tickets online to save big.** ⊠ *Holiday Inn, MM 100 OS, 99701 Overseas Hwy., Key Largo* ☎ *305/451–4655, 877/648–8129* ⊕ *www.keylargoprincess.com* ⊠ *$30.*

CANOEING AND KAYAKING

You can paddle for a few hours or the whole day, on your own or with a guide. Some outfitters even offer overnight trips. The **Florida Keys Overseas Paddling Trail,** part of a statewide system, runs from Key Largo to Key West. You can paddle the entire distance, 106 miles on the Atlantic side, which takes 9 to 10 days.

Coral Reef Park Co.

CANOEING & ROWING | FAMILY | At John Pennekamp Coral Reef State Park, this operator has a fleet of canoes and kayaks for gliding around the 2½-mile mangrove trail or along the coast. Powerboat rentals are also available. ⌧ *MM 102.5 OS, 102601 Overseas Hwy., Key Largo* ☎ *305/451–6300* ⊕ *www.pennekamppark.com* ⌸ *Rentals from $20 per hr.*

Florida Bay Outfitters

CANOEING & ROWING | FAMILY | Rent canoes, sea kayaks, or Hobie Eclipses from this company, which matches equipment to your skill level and also sets up self-guided trips on the Florida Keys Overseas Paddling Trail and helps with trip planning. ⌧ *MM 104 BS, 104050 Overseas Hwy., Key Largo* ☎ *305/451–3018* ⊕ *www. paddlefloridakeys.com* ⌸ *From $15.*

DOLPHIN INTERACTION PROGRAMS

The Keys have several places where you can interact with dolphins. Some people love seeing dolphins up close; others bristle at animals being kept in captivity. If you're among the latter, avoid these programs and instead opt for a dolphin-spotting tour in the wild; just be sure that your tour operator doesn't do anything to attract dolphins to its boats.

FISHING

Sailors Choice

FISHING | Fishing excursions depart twice daily (half-day trips are cash only), but the company also does private charters. The 65-foot boat leaves from the Holiday Inn docks. Rods, bait, and license are included. ⌧ *Holiday Inn Resort and Marina, MM 100 OS, 99701 Overseas Hwy., Key Largo* ☎ *305/451–1802, 305/451–0041* ⊕ *www.sailorschoicefishingboat.com* ⌸ *From $45.*

SCUBA DIVING AND SNORKELING

Amy Slate's Amoray Dive Resort

SCUBA DIVING | This outfit makes diving easy. Stroll down to the full-service dive shop (PADI, TDI, and BSAC certified), then onto a 45-foot catamaran. Certification courses are also offered. ⌧ *MM 104.2 BS, 104250 Overseas Hwy., Key Largo* ☎ *305/451–3595, 800/426–6729* ⊕ *www.amoray.com* ⌸ *From $85.*

Conch Republic Divers

SCUBA DIVING | Book diving instruction as well as scuba and snorkeling tours of Upper Keys wrecks and reefs. Two-location dives are the standard; tanks and weights cost $20 extra. ⊠ *MM 90.8 BS, 90800 Overseas Hwy., Key Largo* ☎ *305/852–1655, 800/274–3483* ⊕ *www.conchrepublicdivers.com* ⌨ *From $80.*

Coral Reef Park Co.

SCUBA DIVING | At John Pennekamp Coral Reef State Park, this company gives 3½-hour scuba and 2½-hour snorkeling tours of the park. In addition to the great location and the dependability, it's also suited for water adventurers of all levels. ⊠ *MM 102.5 OS, 102601 Overseas Hwy., Key Largo* ☎ *305/451–6300* ⊕ *www. pennekamppark.com* ⌨ *From $30.*

Horizon Divers

SCUBA DIVING | Horizon offers customized diving and snorkeling trips aboard a 45-foot catamaran. ⊠ *105.8, 105800 Overseas Hwy., Key Largo* ☎ *305/453–3535, 800/984–3483* ⊕ *www.horizon-divers.com* ⌨ *Snorkeling from $50, diving from $85.*

Island Ventures

SCUBA DIVING | If you like dry British humor and no crowds, this is the operator for you. It specializes in small groups for snorkeling or dive trips, no more than 10 people per boat. Scuba trips are two tanks and two locations and include tanks and weights; ride-alongs pay just $35. Choose morning or afternoon. ⊠ *Jules Undersea Lodge, 51 Shoreland Dr., Key Largo* ☎ *305/451–4957* ⊕ *www.islandventure.com* ⌨ *Snorkel trips $45, diving $85.*

★ Quiescence Diving Services

SCUBA DIVING | This operator limits groups to six to ensure personal attention and offers day, twilight (when sea creatures are most active), and night dives, as well as organized snorkeling excursions. ⊠ *MM 103.5 BS, 103680 Overseas Hwy., Key Largo* ☎ *305/451–2440* ⊕ *keylargodiving.com* ⌨ *Snorkel trips $55, diving from $89.*

Islamorada

Between MM 90.5 and 70.

Early maps show Islamorada as encompassing only Upper Matecumbe Key. But the incorporated "Village of Islands" is made up of a string of islands that the Overseas Highway crosses, including Plantation Key, Windley Key, Upper Matecumbe Key, Lower Matecumbe Key, Craig Key, and Fiesta Key.

Islamorada (locals pronounce it *eye*-la-mor- *ah*-da) is one of the world's top fishing destinations. For nearly 100 years, seasoned anglers have fished these clear, warm waters teeming with trophy-worthy fish. It's also known for sophisticated resorts and restaurants that meet the needs of those in search of luxury, but there's still plenty for those who want something more casual and affordable.

GETTING HERE AND AROUND

Most visitors arrive in Islamorada by car. If you're flying into Miami International Airport or Key West International Airport, you can easily rent a car (reserve in advance) to make the drive.

VISITOR INFORMATION

CONTACT Islamorada Chamber of Commerce & Visitors Center.
✉ *MM 87.1 BS, 87100 Overseas Hwy., Upper Matecumbe Key* ☎ *305/664–4503, 800/322–5397* ⊕ *www.islamoradachamber.com.*

 Sights

Florida Keys Memorial/Hurricane Monument

MONUMENT | On Monday, September 2, 1935, more than 400 people perished when the most intense hurricane to make landfall in the United States swept through this area of the Keys. Two years later, the Florida Keys Memorial was dedicated in their honor. Native coral rock, known as keystone, covers the 18-foot obelisk monument that marks the cremated remains of some 300 of the storm victims. ✉ *MM 81.8, 81831 Old State Hwy. 4A, Upper Matecumbe Key* ⊹ *In front of the public library and just south of the Cheeca Lodge entrance* ⊠ *Free.*

★ Founders Park

CITY PARK | **FAMILY** | Amenities at this gem of a public park include a palm-shaded beach, pool, marina, skate park, tennis, and places to rent a boat or learn to sail. If you're staying in Islamorada, admission is free; otherwise, it costs $8 (cash only) to enter. ✉ *MM 87 BS, 87000 Overseas Hwy., Plantation Key* ☎ *305/853–1685* ⊕ *www.islamorada.fl.us/departments/parks_and_recreation/founders_park.php.*

★ History of Diving Museum

HISTORY MUSEUM | **FAMILY** | This museum plunges into the history of man's thirst for undersea exploration. Amid its 13 galleries of interactive and other interesting displays are a submarine and helmet re-created from the film *20,000 Leagues Under the Sea.* Vintage U.S. Navy equipment, diving helmets from around the world, and early scuba gear explore 4,000 years of diving history. Nifty

Enjoy nautical adventures like boating at family-friendly Robbie's Marina on Islamorada.

scavenger hunt printouts make this fun for little ones. ✉ *MM 83 BS, 82990 Overseas Hwy., Upper Matecumbe Key* ☎ *305/664–9737* ⊕ *www.divingmuseum.org* 🎟 *$15.*

Indian Key Historic State Park

STATE/PROVINCIAL PARK | Mystery surrounds 10-acre Indian Key, on the ocean side of the Matecumbe islands. It was a base for 19th-century shipwreck salvagers until an 1840 attack by Native Americans wiped out the settlement. Dr. Henry Perrine, a noted botanist, was killed in the raid. Today, his plants grow in the town's ruins. Most people kayak or canoe to the park or take a boat from Robbie's Marina to snorkel or explore nature trails and the town ruins. ✉ *Islamorada* ☎ *305/664–2540* ⊕ *www.floridastateparks. org/parks-and-trails/indian-key-historic-state-park* 🎟 *Free.*

Lignumvitae Key Botanical State Park

STATE/PROVINCIAL PARK | On the National Register of Historic Places, this 280-acre bayside island is the site of a virgin hardwood forest and the 1919 home of chemical magnate William Matheson. His caretaker's cottage serves as the park's visitor center. Access is by boat—your own, a rented vessel, or a tour operated from Robbie's Marina. The tour leaves at 8:30 am Friday through Sunday and takes in both Lignumvitae and Indian Key (reservations required). ✉ *Islamorada* ☎ *305/664–2540 park, 305/664–8070 boat tours* ⊕ *www.floridastateparks.org/parks-and-trails/lignumvitae-key-botanical-state-park* 🎟 *$2.50, boat tours $35.*

Robbie's Marina

MARINA/PIER | FAMILY | Silver-sided tarpon—huge, prehistoric-looking denizens of the not-so-deep—congregate around the docks at this authentic local marina. Children (and many adults) pay $4.50 for a bucket of sardines to feed them and $2.50 each for dock admission. You can also grab a bite to eat indoors or out; shop at a slew of artisans' booths; or charter a boat, kayak, or other watercraft. ⊠ *MM 77.5 BS, 77522 Overseas Hwy., Lower Matecumbe Key* ☎ *305/664–8070, 877/664–8498* ⊕ *www.robbies.com.*

Theater of the Sea

OTHER ATTRACTION | FAMILY | The second-oldest marine-mammal center in the world doesn't attempt to compete with more modern, more expensive parks. Even so, it's among the better attractions north of Key West, especially if you have kids in tow. In addition to seeing marine-life exhibits and shows, you can make reservations for up-close-and-personal encounters like a swim with a dolphin or sea lion or stingray and turtle feedings (which include general admission and also require reservations). Stop for lunch at the grill, shop in the extensive gift shop, or sunbathe and swim at the private beach. ⊠ *MM 84.5 OS, 84721 Overseas Hwy., Windley Key* ☎ *305/664–2431* ⊕ *www.theaterofthesea.com* 🖭 *$45, interaction programs from $65.*

Upper Matecumbe Key

ISLAND | This was one of the first of the Upper Keys to be permanently settled. Early homesteaders were so successful at growing pineapples in the rocky soil that, at one time, the island yielded the country's largest annual crop. However, foreign competition and the hurricane of 1935 killed the industry. Today, life centers on fishing and tourism, and the island is filled with everything from bait shops and charter boats to eclectic galleries and fusion restaurants. ⊠ *MM 84–79, Upper Matecumbe Key.*

Windley Key

ISLAND | Originally two islets, this area was first inhabited by Native Americans, who left behind a few traces of their dwellings, and then by farmers and fishermen who built their homes here in the mid-1800s. Henry Flagler bought the land from homesteaders in 1908 for his Florida East Coast Railway, filling in the inlet between what were then called the Umbrella Keys. Today, this is where you'll find Theater of the Sea, the famous Holiday Isle (now Postcard Inn), and Windley Key Fossil Reef Geological State Park. ⊠ *MM 86–84, Windley Key.*

Windley Key Fossil Reef Geological State Park

STATE/PROVINCIAL PARK | FAMILY | The fossilized-coral reef, dating back about 125,000 years, demonstrates that the Florida Keys were once beneath the ocean. Excavation of Windley Key's limestone bed by the Florida East Coast Railway exposed the petrified reef, full of beautifully fossilized brain coral and sea ferns. You can see the fossils along a 300-foot quarry wall when hiking the park's three trails. ✉ *MM 84.9 BS, Windley Key* ☎ *305/664–2540* ⊕ *www.floridastateparks.org/parks-and-trails/windley-key-fossil-reef-geological-state-park* ✍ *$2.50, guided tours $2 (self-guided free)* ⊘ *Closed Tues. and Wed.*

Beaches

Anne's Beach

BEACH | FAMILY | On Lower Matecumbe Key this popular village park is named for a local environmental activist. Its "beach" (really a typical Keys-style sand flat with a gentle slope) is best enjoyed at low tide. The nicest feature here is the elevated, wooden, ½-mile boardwalk that meanders through a natural wetland hammock. Covered picnic areas along the way give you places to linger and enjoy the view. Restrooms are at the north end. Weekends are packed with Miami day-trippers as it's the only public beach until you reach Marathon. **Amenities:** parking (no fee); toilets. **Best for:** partiers; snorkeling; swimming; windsurfing. ✉ *MM 73.5 OS, Lower Matecumbe Key* ☎ *305/853–1685.*

🍴 Restaurants

Bitton Bistro Café

$ | **FRENCH** | Authentic French food is on the menu at this super-casual eatery run by chef-owner Michel Bitton. The gelatos and homemade French pastries might be famous, but don't miss the opportunity to savor his daily quiches, fresh salads with Dijon vinaigrette, rustic soups, and French baguette sandwiches. **Known for:** oversize crepes; freshly made gelato; wide assortment of macarons. ⑤ *Average main: $12* ✉ *MM 82 OS, 82245 Overseas Hwy., Upper Matecumbe Key* ☎ *305/396–7481* ⊕ *facebook.com/BittonBistroCafe* ▭ *No credit cards* ⊘ *No dinner.*

★ Chef Michael's

$$$$ | **SEAFOOD** | This local favorite makes big waves with fresh seafood that's prepared with tropical flair. Carnivores can feast on prime-grade beef, which is carved in-house and has the kind of marbling that just melts in your mouth. **Known for:** watermelon mint sangria; fresh catch "Juliette" with shrimp and scallops; intimate tropical dining. ⑤ *Average main: $38* ✉ *MM 81.7, 81671 Overseas Hwy., Upper Matecumbe Key* ☎ *305/664–0640* ⊕ *www.foodtotalkabout.com* ⊘ *No lunch Mon.–Sat.*

Green Turtle Inn

$$ | SEAFOOD | This circa-1947 landmark—with its vintage neon sign, wood-paneled walls, and period photos—is a slice of Florida Keys history. Breakfast options include French toast made with challah bread and Captain Morgan batter or Keys Benedict with a blue crab cake; at lunch, opt for lobster mac and cheese. **Known for:** excellent conch chowder; outstanding pound cake; huge homemade sticky buns. ⑤ *Average main: $24* ⊠ *MM 81.2 OS, 81219 Overseas Hwy., Upper Matecumbe Key* ☎ *305/664–2006* ⊕ *www.greenturtlekeys.com* ⊘ *Closed Mon.*

Hungry Tarpon

$ | SEAFOOD | FAMILY | This is part of the colorful, bustling Old Florida scene at Robbie's Marina, so you know that the seafood here is fresh and top quality. The extensive menu seems as if it's bigger than the dining space, which consists of a few tables and counter seating indoors, plus tables out back under the mangrove trees. **Known for:** insanely good Bloody Marys with a beef-stick straw; heart-of-the-action location; biscuits and gravy. ⑤ *Average main: $19* ⊠ *MM 77.5 BS, 77522 Overseas Hwy., Lower Matecumbe Key* ☎ *305/664–0535* ⊕ *www.hungrytarpon.com.*

Islamorada Fish Company

$ | SEAFOOD | FAMILY | Owned by Bass Pro Shops and housed in an open-air, oversize tiki hut on Florida Bay, this restaurant offers a quintessential Keys dining experience. Menu highlights include cracked conch beaten till tender and then fried and fresh-catch Portofino blackened perfectly and topped with Key West shrimp and a brandied lobster sauce. **Known for:** tourist hot spot; great views; afternoon fish and shark feedings in its private lagoon. ⑤ *Average main: $18* ⊠ *MM 81.5 BS, 81532 Overseas Hwy., Upper Matecumbe Key* ☎ *305/664–9271* ⊕ *www.islamoradafish-co.com.*

Island Grill

$ | SEAFOOD | Don't be fooled by appearances; this waterfront shack takes island breakfast, lunch, and dinner up a notch. Tempting options include the famed "original tuna nachos," lobster rolls, and a nice selection of seafood and sandwiches. **Known for:** eclectic seafood options; slow service; nice views. ⑤ *Average main: $14* ⊠ *MM 85.5 OS, 85501 Overseas Hwy., Islamorada* ☎ *305/664–8400* ⊕ *www.keysislandgrill.com.*

Kaiyo Grill & Sushi

$$$ | JAPANESE | Colorful abstract mosaics and inviting, upholstered banquettes almost steal the show, but the food is equally interesting. The menu, a fusion of East and West, offers sushi rolls that combine local ingredients with traditional Japanese tastes. **Known for:** drunken scallops; showstopping decor; dessert cupcakes that look like sushi. $ *Average main: $35* ✉ *MM 81.5 OS, 81701 Overseas Hwy., Upper Matecumbe Key* ☎ *305/664–5556* ⊙ *Closed Sun. and Mon. No lunch.*

Marker 88

$$$ | SEAFOOD | A few yards from Florida Bay, this popular seafood restaurant has large picture windows that offer great sunset views, though most patrons dine outside on the sand. Chef Bobby Stoky serves such irresistible entrées as onion-crusted mahimahi and house-smoked sea-salt-and-black-pepper-encrusted rib eye. **Known for:** a gathering place for locals and visitors; fantastic fresh-fish sandwich; extensive wine list. $ *Average main: $34* ✉ *MM 88 BS, 88000 Overseas Hwy., Plantation Key* ☎ *305/852–9315* ⊕ *www.marker88.info.*

Morada Bay Beach Café

$$$ | ECLECTIC | FAMILY | This bayfront restaurant wins high marks for its surprisingly stellar cuisine, tables in the sand, and tiki torches that bathe the evening in romance. Seafood takes center stage, but you can always get roasted organic chicken or prime rib. **Known for:** feet-in-the-sand dining; full-moon parties; intoxicating sunset views. $ *Average main: $27* ✉ *MM 81 BS, 81600 Overseas Hwy., Upper Matecumbe Key* ☎ *305/664–0604* ⊕ *www.moradabay.com.*

★ Pierre's Restaurant

$$$$ | FRENCH | One of the Keys' most elegant restaurants, Pierre's marries colonial style with modern food trends and lets you taste the world from its romantic verandas. French chocolate, Australian lamb, Hawaiian fish, Florida lobster—whatever is fresh and in season will be masterfully prepared and beautifully served. **Known for:** romantic spot for that special night out; seasonally changing menu; full-moon parties. $ *Average main: $43* ✉ *MM 81.5 BS, 81600 Overseas Hwy., Upper Matecumbe Key* ☎ *305/664–3225* ⊕ *www.moradabay.com* ⊙ *No lunch.*

☕ Coffee and Quick Bites

Bayside Gourmet

$ | ITALIAN | FAMILY | This tiny counter-service restaurant is the best-kept secret in Islamorada, with the tastiest and most affordable ($11) grouper Reuben sandwich in the Keys. It's a small place—with six tables inside, a bar overlooking the kitchen, and an outdoor patio—and most diners are locals. **Known for:** excellent key lime pie; microbrews; seafood omelets. $ *Average main: $17*

✉ *MM 82.7 BS, 82758 Overseas Hwy., Upper Matecumbe Key* ☎ *305/735–4471* ⊕ *baysidegourmet.com.*

Hotels

Amara Cay Resort

$$ | RESORT | At this simple yet chic resort, spacious rooms evoke well-to-do bachelor pads, complete with a counter and stools, wine chiller, minimalistic furniture, and artwork. **Pros:** free local shuttle; use of kayaks, bikes, paddleboards; oceanfront zero-entry pool. **Cons:** pricey $40 daily resort fee; living areas of rooms lack seating; no on-site spa. ⑤ *Rooms from: $299* ✉ *MM 80 OS, 80001 Overseas Hwy., Upper Matecumbe Key* ☎ *305/664–0073* ⊕ *www.amaracayresort.com* ⌦ *110 rooms* ⚭ *No Meals.*

Casa Morada

$$$ | B&B/INN | This relic from the 1950s has been restyled into a suave, design-forward, all-suites property with outdoor showers and whirlpool tubs in some of the suites. **Pros:** private island connected by footbridge; adults only; complimentary use of bikes, kayaks, paddleboards, and snorkel gear. **Cons:** dinner off property; beach is small and inconsequential; minimum two-night stay on weekends. ⑤ *Rooms from: $400* ✉ *MM 82 BS, 136 Madeira Rd., Upper Matecumbe Key* ☎ *305/664–0044, 888/881–3030* ⊕ *www. casamorada.com* ⌦ *16 suites* ⚭ *Free Breakfast.*

★ Cheeca Lodge & Spa

$$$$ | RESORT | FAMILY | One of the most storied and luxurious resorts in the Keys, this legendary property still packs in more amenities than any other we can think of. **Pros:** everything you need is on site; designer rooms; water-sports center on property. **Cons:** expensive rates; expensive resort fee; can get busy. ⑤ *Rooms from: $410* ✉ *MM 82 OS, 81801 Overseas Hwy., Upper Matecumbe Key* ☎ *305/664–4651, 800/327–2888* ⊕ *www.cheeca. com* ⌦ *214 rooms* ⚭ *No Meals.*

Chesapeake Beach Resort

$$ | RESORT | FAMILY | Modern conveniences and a retro look are among the hallmarks of this boutique hotel on the beach. **Pros:** oceanfront location; reasonable prices; private porches or balconies. **Cons:** no dining on site; $25 resort fee per night; no spa. ⑤ *Rooms from: $210* ✉ *MM 83.5, 83409 Overseas Hwy., Upper Matecumbe Key* ☎ *305/664–4662, 800/338–3395* ⊕ *www.chesapeake-resort.com* ⌦ *52 rooms* ⚭ *No Meals.*

Drop Anchor

$$ | HOTEL | Immaculately maintained, this place has the feel of an old friend's beach house, and it's easy to find the one- or two-bedroom units, as they are painted in an array of Crayola colors. **Pros:** bright and colorful; very clean; laid-back charm. **Cons:** noise from the highway; beach is for fishing, not swimming; simplicity isn't for everyone. $ *Rooms from: $200* ✉ *MM 85 OS, 84959 Overseas Hwy., Windley Key* ☎ *305/664–4863, 888/664–4863* ⊕ *www.dropanchorresort.com* ⌁ *18 suites* ⦿ *No Meals.*

Islander Resort

$$ | **RESORT** | **FAMILY** | Here you get to choose between a self-sufficient town home on the bay side or an oceanfront resort with on-site restaurants and oodles of other amenities. **Pros:** spacious rooms; nice kitchens; eye-popping views. **Cons:** pricey; no dining at bayside location; some activities have a fee. $ *Rooms from: $300* ✉ *MM 82.1 OS, 82200 Overseas Hwy., Upper Matecumbe Key* ☎ *305/664–0082* ⊕ *www.islanderfloridakeys.com* ⌁ *114 rooms* ⦿ *No Meals.*

★ The Islands of Islamorada

$$$ | **HOTEL** | Situated right on the Atlantic, this luxury club resort has waterfront villas and hotel suites, all nestled along 600 feet of private shoreline. **Pros:** private marina; luxurious facilities and amenities; 24-hour gym. **Cons:** limited number of units means it's often booked solid; luxury comes at a price; lacks a full-service restaurant. $ *Rooms from: $399* ✉ *MM 82 OS, 82885 Old Hwy., Windley Key* ☎ *866/540–5520* ⊕ *theislandsofislamorada.com* ⌁ *30 units* ⦿ *Free Breakfast.*

La Siesta Resort & Marina

$$$ | **RESORT** | **FAMILY** | With 6 acres of oceanfront property, accommodations that range from studio units to a glamorous three-bedroom waterfront home, and staffers who go the extra mile, this resort has everything a visitor to the Keys could want. **Pros:** free use of kayaks, paddleboards, bicycles, and fishing rods; free Wi-Fi; access to sister properties. **Cons:** $40 nightly resort fee; bar-café only open till 7; not a swimming beach. $ *Rooms from: $399* ✉ *MM 80.2 OS, 80241 Overseas Hwy., Upper Matecumbe Key* ☎ *305/664–2132, 855/335–1078 reservations* ⊕ *www.lasiestaresort.com* ⌁ *53 rooms* ⦿ *Free Breakfast.*

Little Basin Villas

$$$$ | **HOTEL** | **FAMILY** | These two-story, state-of-the-art, 1,600-square-foot villas could easily be the set for a *Coastal Living* magazine shoot. **Pros:** great location; nice pool and tiki huts; floating dock for launching kayaks. **Cons:** no office on site; mangroves block full water views; no daily housekeeping. $ *Rooms from: $550* ✉ *MM 81.8 BS, 84 Johnson Rd., Upper Matecumbe Key* ⌖ *Next to the Islamorada Public Library* ☎ *305/363–8999* ⊕ *littlebasinvillas.com* ⌁ *9 villas* ⦿ *No Meals.*

The Moorings Village

$$$$ | **HOTEL** | At this tropical retreat, the embodiment of the laid-back Keys, hammocks sway between towering trees and aqua-green waves lap manicured sand. **Pros:** romantic setting; good dining options with room-charging privileges; beautiful views. **Cons:** no room service; $25 daily resort fee for activities; must cross the highway to walk or drive to its restaurants. $ *Rooms from: $800* ⊠ *MM 81.6 OS, 123 Beach Rd., Upper Matecumbe Key* ☎ *305/664–4708* ⊕ *www.themooringsvillage.com* ⇥ *17 cottages* ⦿ *No Meals.*

Postcard Inn Beach Resort & Marina

$$ | **RESORT** | The boathouse-chic units at this storied property have white wooden accents, faux-wood–tiled floors, and a comfy day-bed. **Pros:** large private beach; heated pools; on-site restaurants, including Ciao Hound Italian Kitchen & Bar. **Cons:** rooms near tiki bar are noisy; minimum stay required during peak times; some rooms overlook a parking lot. $ *Rooms from: $267* ⊠ *MM 84 OS, 84001 Overseas Hwy., Islamorada* ☎ *305/664–2321* ⊕ *www. holidayisle.com* ⇥ *145 rooms* ⦿ *No Meals.*

Ragged Edge Resort & Marina

$$ | **HOTEL** | **FAMILY** | Nicely tucked away in a residential area at the ocean's edge, this family-owned hotel draws returning guests who'd rather fish off the dock and grill up dinner than loll around on Egyptian-cotton sheets. **Pros:** oceanfront setting; boat docks and ramp; cheap rates for Islamorada. **Cons:** dated decor; off the beaten path; not within walking distance of anything. $ *Rooms from: $209* ⊠ *MM 86.5 OS, 243 Treasure Harbor Rd., Plantation Key* ☎ *305/852–5389, 800/436–2023* ⊕ *www.ragged-edge.com* ⇥ *10 units* ⦿ *No Meals.*

Nightlife

Hog Heaven

BARS | Come by boat or car to this oceanfront restaurant and sports bar, where you can soak in the views dockside or relax in the air-conditioning. Munch on fresh fish sandwiches or barbecue dishes while you shoot pool, catch the big game on large flat-screens, or dance to a live band or DJ. Late night can get a bit wild and loud. ⊠ *MM 85.3 OS, 85361 Overseas Hwy., Windley Key* ☎ *305/664–9669* ⊕ *www.hogheavensportsbar.com.*

The Lorelei Restaurant and Cabana Bar

BARS | A larger-than-life mermaid guides you to the kind of place you fantasize about during those long, cold winters up north. It's all about good drinks, tasty pub grub, and beautiful sunsets set to live bands playing island tunes and light rock nightly. Dining is all outdoors, on a deck or under the trees. Service is slow, sometimes even nonexistent. ⊠ *MM 82 BS, 81924 Overseas Hwy., Upper Matecumbe Key* ☎ *305/664–2692* ⊕ *www.loreleicabanabar.com.*

Ziggie & Mad Dog's

BARS | The area's glam celebrity hangout, Ziggie & Mad Dog's serves appetizers with its happy-hour drink specials. Its wine list and outrageous steaks have become legendary. ⊠ *MM 83 BS, 83000 Overseas Hwy., Upper Matecumbe Key* ☎ *305/004–0091* ⊕ *www.ziggieandmaddogs.com.*

Shopping

GALLERIES

Pasta Pantaleo's Signature Gallery

ART GALLERIES | Roberto Pantaleo, better known as "Pasta," is one of the Keys' best-known (and widely collected) artists. His subjects range from vibrant turtles to subtle seas and mangroves. His work can also be seen in the local Roberto • Russell Galleries. ⊠ *81599 Old Hwy., Upper Matecumbe Key* ⊹ *Downtown Islamorada in the Morada Way Art District* ☎ *305/619–9924* ⊕ *www.artbypasta.com.*

Rain Barrel Village

CRAFTS | You can't miss the giant sculpture of Betsy the lobster in front of this eclectic spot. Set in a tropical garden of shady trees, native shrubs, and orchids, the crafts village has shops selling the work of local and national artists, as well as resident artists who sell work from their own studios. ⊠ *MM 86.7 BS, 86700 Overseas Hwy., Plantation Key* ☎ *305/852–3084* ⊕ *rainbarrelvillage.com.*

Redbone Gallery

CRAFTS | This gallery stocks hand-stitched clothing, giftware, and jewelry, in addition to works of art by watercolorists C. D. Clarke and Julie Joyce and painters Luther Hall, Stephen Left, Tim Borski, and Jorge Martinez, among others. Proceeds benefit cystic fibrosis research. It's in the Morada Way Arts and Cultural District. ⊠ *MM 81.5 OS, 200 Morada Way, Upper Matecumbe Key* ☎ *305/664–2002* ⊕ *www.redbone.org.*

GIFTS

The Banyan Tree Garden & Boutique

OTHER SPECIALTY STORE | Lush grounds, unique gifts, and free-spirited clothing are among the draws at this boutique. ⊠ *MM 81.2 OS, 81197 Overseas Hwy., Upper Matecumbe Key* ☎ *305/664–3433* ⊕ *www.banyantreeboutique.com.*

Ocean Gardens

ANTIQUES & COLLECTIBLES | Warning: you could spend hours in here and drop some serious cash on the one-of-a-kind home-decor pieces and marine antiques. It's more than a shop; it's a showroom of all things upscale nautical. Come browse and be amazed. ⊠ MM 82.2 OS, 82237 Overseas Hwy., Upper Matecumbe Key ☎ 305/664–2793 ⊕ www.oceangardensandgifts.com.

Olive Morada

FOOD | This place has more than a clever name: you'll find a nice assortment of top-quality imported olive oils and specialty and balsamic vinegars that will delight your taste buds and turn you on to flavors and combos you never imagined. Try Sicilian-lemon olive oil with blood-orange vinegar on an avocado salad. Or, try scrambling your eggs in Tuscan-herb olive oil. Tastings are encouraged. Pastas, crackers, spices, and a variety of kitchen-inspired gifts adorn the shelves as well. ⊠ 82229 Overseas Hwy., Upper Matecumbe Key ☎ 305/735–4375 ⊕ www.olivemorada.com.

JEWELRY

Blue Marlin Jewelry

JEWELRY & WATCHES | For more than 20 years, this family-owned and-operated jeweler has been adding unique sparkle and shine to the lives of visitors and locals alike. At the premier jeweler in the Keys, you will find nautical- and tropical-themed jewelry as well as high-end pens, pocket knives, and money clips that are functional art. ⊠ MM 81.5 OS, 81549 Old Hwy., Upper Matecumbe Key ☎ 305/664–8004 ⊕ www.bluemarlinjewelry.com.

SHOPPING CENTERS

★ Casa Mar Village

MALL | What was once a row of worn-down buildings is now a merry mix of gift shops and galleries. By day, these colorful stores glisten at their canal-front location; by nightfall, they're lit up like a lovely Christmas town. ⊠ MM 90 OS, 90775 Old Hwy., Plantation Key ⊕ www.casamarvillage.com.

Village Square at the Trading Post

NEIGHBORHOODS | This shopping village has garden alcoves, picnic tables, and shops with everything from trendy clothing and artwork to home decor. The Bohemian Arts Club hosts classes and other events here. Grab a bite at Bad Boy Burrito, where the fish tacos are almost legendary. ⊠ MM 81.8 BS, 81868 Overseas Hwy., Upper Matecumbe Key ☎ 305/440–3951 ⊕ www.villagesquareislamorada.com.

SPORTING GOODS
Bass Pro Shops - World Wide Sportsman
SPORTING GOODS | This two-level retail center sells upscale and everyday fishing equipment, resort clothing, sport-fishing art, and other gifts. It's worth a stop to climb aboard the *Pilar,* a replica of Hemingway's boat installed in the middle of the store. ⊠ *MM 81.5 BS, 81576 Overseas Hwy., Upper Matecumbe Key* ☎ *305/664–4615, 800/327–2880* ⊕ *www.basspro.com.*

 # Activities

BOATING
Early Bird Fishing Charters
FISHING | Captain Ross knows these waters well, and he'll hook you up with whatever is in season—mahimahi, sailfish, tuna, and wahoo, to name a few—while you cruise on a comfy and stylish 43-foot custom Willis charter boat. The salon is air-conditioned for those hot summer days, and everything but booze and food is included. ⊠ *Bud N' Mary's Marina, MM 79.8 OS, 79851 Overseas Hwy., Upper Matecumbe Key* ☎ *305/942–3618* ⊕ *www.fishearly-bird.com* ⟟ *4 hrs $850, 6 hrs $1,100, 8 hrs $1,300.*

Keys Boat Rental
BOATING | You can rent both fishing and deck boats here (from 18 to 29 feet) by the day or the week. Free local delivery with seven-day rentals from each of its locations is available. ⊠ *MM 85.9 BS and 99.7 OS, 85920 Overseas Hwy., Plantation Key* ☎ *305/664–9404, 877/453–9463* ⊕ *www.keysboatrental.com* ⟟ *Rentals from $240 per day.*

Robbie's Boat Rentals
BOATING | This full-service company will even give you a crash course on how not to crash your boat. The rental fleet includes an 18-foot skiff with a 90-horsepower outboard and a 21-foot deck boat with a 130-horsepower engine. Robbie's also rents snorkeling gear (there's good snorkeling nearby) and sells bait, drinks, and snacks. Want to hire a guide who knows the local waters and where the fish lurk? Robbie's offers offshore-fishing trips, patch-reef trips, and party-boat fishing. Backcountry flats trips are a specialty. ⊠ *MM 77.5 BS, 77522 Overseas Hwy., Lower Matecumbe Key* ☎ *305/664–9814, 877/664–8498* ⊕ *www.robbies.com* ⟟ *From $185 per day.*

FISHING
★ Bamboo Charters
FISHING | A world-class fisherman and guide who studied to be a marine biologist, Captain Matt know his stuff, whether you want

a calm day in the shallow waters or a day at the reef catching snapper, grouper, or anything else with fins. ⊠ *Angler House Marina MM 80.5, 80500 Overseas Hwy., Upper Matecumbe Key* ☎ *305/394–0000* ⊕ *www.bamboocharters.com.*

Captain Ted Wilson

FISHING | Go into the backcountry for bonefish, tarpon, redfish, snook, and shark aboard a 17-foot boat that accommodates up to three anglers. Choose four-, six-, or eight-hour trips or evening tarpon-fishing excursions. Rates are for one or two anglers. There's a $75 charge for an additional person. ⊠ *Bud N' Mary's Marina, MM 79.9 OS, 79851 Overseas Hwy., Upper Matecumbe Key* ☎ *305/942–5224* ⊕ *www.captaintedwilson.com* ⊠ *Half-day and evening trips from $450.*

Florida Keys Fly Fish

FISHING | Like other top fly-fishing and light-tackle guides, Captain Geoff Colmes helps his clients land trophy fish in the waters around the Keys, from Islamorada to Flamingo in the Everglades. ⊠ *105 Palm La., Plantation Key* ☎ *305/393–1245* ⊕ *www.florida-keysflyfish.com* ⊠ *From $550.*

Florida Keys Outfitters

FISHING | Long before fly-fishing became popular, Sandy Moret was fishing the Keys for bonefish, tarpon, and redfish. Now he attracts anglers from around the world on a quest for the big catch. ⊠ *Green Turtle, MM 81.2, 81219 Overseas Hwy., Upper Matecumbe Key* ☎ *305/664–5423* ⊕ *www.floridakeysoutfitters. com* ⊠ *Half-day trips from $550.*

Miss Islamorada

FISHING | This 65-foot party boat offers full-day fishing trips. Bring your lunch or buy one from the dockside deli. ⊠ *Bud N' Mary's Marina, MM 79.8 OS, 79851 Overseas Hwy., Upper Matecumbe Key* ☎ *305/664–2461, 800/742–7945* ⊕ *www.budnmarys.com* ⊠ *$70.*

KAYAKING

The Kayak Shack

KAYAKING | You can rent kayaks for trips to Indian Key (about 20 minutes one-way) and Lignumvitae Key (about 45 minutes one-way), two favorite destinations for paddlers. ⊠ *Robbie's Marina, MM 77.5 BS, 77522 Overseas Hwy., Lower Matecumbe Key* ☎ *305/664–4878* ⊕ *www.kayakthefloridakeys.com* ⊠ *From $40 for single, $55 for double; guided trips from $45.*

SCUBA DIVING AND SNORKELING
Florida Keys Dive Center
SCUBA DIVING | Dive from John Pennekamp Coral Reef State Park to Alligator Reef with this outfitter. It has two 46-foot Coast Guard–approved dive boats, offers scuba training, and is one of the few Keys dive centers to offer nitrox and trimix (mixed-gas) diving. ⊠ *MM 90.5 OS, 90451 Overseas Hwy., Plantation Key* ☎ *305/852–4599, 800/433–8946* ⊕ *www.floridakeysdivecenter. com* ⊠ *Snorkeling from $38, diving from $84.*

Islamorada Dive Center
SCUBA DIVING | This one-stop dive shop has a resort, pool, restaurant, lessons, twice-daily dive and snorkel trips, and the newest fleet in the Keys. Take a day-trip with a two-tank dive or a one-tank night trip with their equipment or yours. Snorkel and spearfishing trips are also available. ⊠ *MM 84 OS, 84001 Overseas Hwy., Windley Key* ☎ *305/664–3483, 800/327–7070* ⊕ *www.islamora-dadivecenter.com* ⊠ *Snorkel trips from $45, diving from $85.*

San Pedro Underwater Archaeological Preserve State Park
SCUBA DIVING | This site includes the remains of a Spanish treasure-fleet ship that sank in 1733. Resting in only 18 feet of water, its ruins are visible to snorkelers as well as divers and attract a colorful array of fish. ⊠ *MM 85.5 OS, Islamorada* ☎ *305/664–2540* ⊕ *www.floridastateparks.org/parks-and-trails/ san-pedro-underwater-archaeological-preserve-state-park.*

Long Key

Between MM 70 and 65.5.

Long Key isn't a tourist hot spot, so it's favored by those who want to avoid the masses and enjoy natural history.

Sights

Layton Nature Trail
TRAIL | FAMILY | Up the road about ½ mile from Long Key State Park, beginning at a close-to-the-ground marker, is a free trail that leads through a tropical-hardwood forest to a rocky Florida Bay shoreline overlooking shallow grass flats. It takes about 20 minutes to walk the ¼-mile route. ⊠ *MM 67.7 BS, Long Key* ⊠ *Free.*

★ Long Key State Park

STATE/PROVINCIAL PARK | FAMILY | Come here for solitude, hiking, and fishing. On the ocean side, the 1.1-mile Golden Orb Trail leads to a boardwalk that cuts through the mangroves (may require some wading) and alongside a lagoon where waterfowl congregate. A 1¼-mile canoe trail leads through a tidal lagoon, and the grass flats are perfect for bonefishing. Bring a mask and snorkel to observe the marine life in the shallow water. ⊠ *MM 67.5 OS, 67400 Overseas Hwy., Long Key* ☎ *305/664–4815* ⊕ *www.floridastateparks.org/park/Long-Key* ⊴ *$4.50 for 1 person, $5.50 for 2 people, and 50¢ for each additional person in the group.*

Long Key Viaduct

BRIDGE | As you cross the Long Key Channel, look beside you at the old viaduct. The second-longest bridge on the former rail line, this 2¼-mile-long structure has 222 reinforced-concrete arches. The old bridge is popular with cyclists and joggers. Anglers fish off the sides day and night. ⊠ *Long Key.*

Beaches

★ Long Key State Park Beach

BEACH | Camping, snorkeling, and bonefishing are popular activities along this narrow strip of natural, rocky shoreline. The day area offers a nice respite, and the campground is edged by shallow, sea-grass-bottom waters. **Amenities:** showers; toilets. **Best for:** snorkeling; swimming; walking. ⊠ *MM 67.5 OS, 67400 Overseas Hwy., Long Key* ☎ *305/664–4815* ⊕ *www.floridastateparks.org/park/Long-Key* ⊴ *$4.50 for 1 person, $5.50 for 2 people, and 50¢ for each additional person in the group.*

Hotels

Lime Tree Bay Resort

$$ | RESORT | FAMILY | Easy on the eye and the wallet, this 2½-acre, Florida Bay resort offers simple accommodations far from the bustle of the larger islands. **Pros:** great views; friendly staff; close to Long Key State Park. **Cons:** limited dock space; shared balconies; $25 daily resort fee. ⑤ *Rooms from: $210* ⊠ *MM 68.5 BS, 68500 Overseas Hwy., Long Key* ☎ *305/664–4740, 800/723–4519* ⊕ *www.limetreebayresort.com* ⇄ *48 units* ⏇ *Free Breakfast.*

THE MIDDLE KEYS

Updated by
Sara Liss

⊙ Sights	🍴 Restaurants	🛏 Hotels	🛍 Shopping	🍸 Nightlife
★★★☆☆	★★★★★	★★★★★	★★★★☆	★★★★☆

WELCOME TO THE MIDDLE KEYS

TOP REASONS TO GO

★ **Crane Point:** Visit 63-acre Crane Point Museum, Nature Center, and Historic Site in Marathon for a primer on local natural and social history.

★ **Beach for the whole family:** Sun, swim, and play with abandon at Marathon's family-oriented Sombrero Beach.

★ **Pigeon Key.** Step into the era of railroad building with a ferry ride to Pigeon Key's historic village, which was once a residential camp for workers on Henry Flagler's Overseas Railroad.

★ **Dolphins:** Kiss a dolphin, and maybe even watch one paint, at Dolphin Research Center, which was begun by the maker of the movie *Flipper.*

★ **Fishing:** Anglers will be happy to hear that the deep-water fishing off Marathon is superb in both the bay and the ocean.

1 Conch Key and Duck Key.
Once used by the Florida East Coast Railway as a construction campsite, sleepy Conch Key is now mainly a place to fish and enjoy water sports, like kayaking and stand-up paddleboarding. Upscale Duck Key is home to renowned Hawks Cay Resort, a 60-acre Caribbean-style resort with several restaurants and a dolphin program. Scuba diving, snorkeling, and sunset cruises are other popular activities.

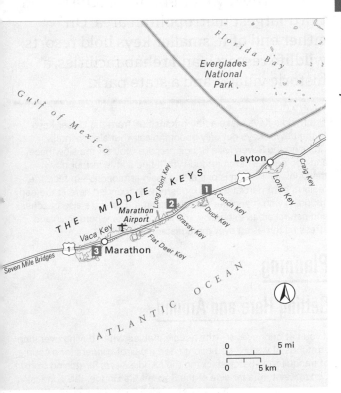

2 Grassy Key. This small key, next to Marathon, is located in the center of the Middle Keys. The major draws include Dolphin Research Center and Curry Hammock State Park, which offers 260 acres of hardwood hammocks (stands of trees), wetlands, and mangroves.

3 Marathon. Marathon's roots are in fishing and boating, so expect to find numerous marinas in this bustling Florida Keys town. In addition to family-friendly activities, you'll find Sombrero Beach, with shaded picnic areas, water sports galore, and plenty of seafood restaurants.

Most activity in the Middle Keys revolves around the town of Marathon, the region's third-largest metropolitan area. On either end of it, smaller keys hold resorts, wildlife research and rehab facilities, a historic village, and a state park.

The Middle Keys make a fitting transition from the Upper Keys to the Lower Keys not only geographically but also mentally. Crossing the Seven Mile Bridge prepares you for the slow pace and don't-give-a-damn attitude you'll find a little farther down the highway. Fishing is one of the main attractions—in fact, the region's commercial fishing industry was founded here in the early 1800s. Diving is another popular pastime. There are also beaches and natural areas to enjoy in the Middle Keys, where mainland stress becomes an ever more distant memory.

Planning

Getting Here and Around

If you get bridge fever—the heebie-jeebies when driving over long stretches of water—you might need a pair of blinders (or a couple of tranquilizers) before tackling the Middle Keys. Stretching from Conch Key to the far side of the Seven Mile Bridge, this zone is home to the region's two longest bridges: Long Key Viaduct and Seven Mile Bridge, both historic landmarks.

To get to the Middle Keys you can fly into either Miami International Airport (MIA) or Key West International Airport (EYW). Key West is closer, but it has far fewer flights. Rental cars are available at both airports. In addition, Key West Transit buses run ($4 one way) from the Key West airport. SuperShuttle charges $300 for up to 11 passengers from MIA to Big Pine Key. Keys Shuttle charges $70 per passenger from MIA to Marathon. You can also take an Uber from MIA to Marathon for about $140.

U.S. 1 traverses the region in a direct line that takes in most of the sights, but you'll find some interesting resorts and restaurants off the main drag.

Hotels

From quaint old cottages to newly built town-house communities, the Middle Keys have it all, often with prices that are more affordable than at the chain's extremes. Hawks Cay has the region's best selection of lodgings.

Restaurants

Hope you're not tired of seafood, because the run of fish houses continues in the Middle Keys. In fact, Marathon has some of the best. Several are not so easy to find but worth the search because of their local color and water views. Expect casual and friendly service with a side of sass. Restaurants may close for two to four weeks during the slow season between September and mid-November, so call ahead if you have a particular place in mind.

Hotel and restaurant reviews have been shortened. For full information, visit Fodors.com. Hotel prices are the lowest cost of a standard double room in high season. Restaurant prices are the average cost of a main course at dinner or, if dinner is not served, at lunch.

What It Costs			
$	$$	$$$	$$$$
RESTAURANTS			
under $20	$20–$25	$26–$35	over $35
HOTELS			
under $200	$200–$300	$301–$400	over $400

Conch Key and Duck Key

Conch Key: between MM 63 and 60. Duck Key: at MM 61.

Fishing dominates Conch Key's economy, and many residents are descendants of immigrants from the mainland South. There are a few lodging options here for those exploring Marathon or taking advantage of the water sports on the more upscale Duck Key, which is just across the causeway from Conch Key and has one of the region's nicest marina resorts, Hawks Cay, as well as a boating-oriented residential community.

🍴 Restaurants

★ Angler & Ale

$$$ | SEAFOOD | FAMILY | If you're a fan of vibrant coastal decor and fresh local seafood, you'll gush over this restaurant and bar overlooking the water and Hawks Cay Marina. The menu is varied with options that include burgers as well as grilled fish, the cocktails are creative, and there are more than a dozen beers on tap. **Known for:** locally sourced seafood like grouper cheeks and Key West pink shrimp; pricey menu; family friendliness. ⑤ *Average main: $30* ⊠ *Hawks Cay Resort, MM 61 OS, 540 Duck Key Dr., Duck Key* ☎ *305/209–9991* ⊕ *www.hawkscay.com.*

Sixty-One Prime

$$$$ | AMERICAN | This elegant, fine-dining restaurant in Hawks Cay Resort serves steaks and seafood. Chefs work with local farmers and fishermen to find what's fresh and in season, then create a menu that will wow your palate (and your wallet). **Known for:** naturally raised certified Black Angus beef; nightly changing menu; attentive service. ⑤ *Average main: $36* ⊠ *Hawks Cay Resort, MM 61 OS, 61 Hawks Cay Blvd., Duck Key* ☎ *305/743–7000, 888/432–2242* ⊕ *www.hawkscay.com* ⊘ *No lunch.*

🛏️ Hotels

★ Hawks Cay Resort

$$$ | RESORT | FAMILY | The 60-acre, Caribbean-style retreat with a full-service spa and six restaurants has plenty to keep the kids occupied (and adults happy). **Pros:** great activities for families; restful spa; full-service marina and dive shop. **Cons:** no real beach; far from Marathon's attractions; resort-wide tram gets busy, so plan to wait or walk far. ⑤ *Rooms from: $315* ⊠ *MM 61 OS, 61 Hawks Cay Blvd., Duck Key* ☎ *305/743–7000, 888/432–2242* ⊕ *www. hawkscay.com* ⇌ *431 units* ⦿ *No Meals.*

🏃 Activities

BOATING

Fish 'n Fun

BOATING | Get out on the water on 19- to 26-foot powerboats. Rentals can be for a half or full day. The company also offers free delivery in the Middle Keys. ⊠ *Duck Key Marina, MM 61 OS, 1149 Greenbriar Rd., Duck Key* ☎ *305/743–2275, 800/471–3440* ⊕ *www.fishnfunrentals.com* ⛴ *From $225.*

DOLPHIN INTERACTION
Dolphin Connection
OTHER ATTRACTION | FAMILY | Hawks Cay Resort's Dolphin Connection offers three programs, including Dockside Dolphins, a 30-minute encounter from the dry training docks; Dolphin Discovery, an in-water program that lasts about 45 minutes and lets you kiss, touch, and feed the dolphins; and Trainer for a Day, a three-hour session with the animal training team. ⊠ *Hawks Cay Resort, MM 61 OS, 61 Hawks Cay Blvd., Duck Key* ☎ *305/289–9975* ⊕ *www. dolphinconnection.com* ⌨ *From $70.*

Grassy Key

Between MM 60 and 57.

Local lore has it that this sleepy little key was named not for its vegetation—mostly native trees and shrubs—but for an early settler by the name of Grassy. A few families operating small fishing camps and roadside motels primarily inhabit the key. Although there's no marked definition between Marathon and Grassy Key, making it feel sort of like a suburb, sights tend toward the natural, including a worthwhile dolphin attraction and a small state park.

GETTING HERE AND AROUND
Most visitors arrive by air and drive here from Miami International or Key West International Airports. Rental cars are readily available at both and, in the long run, are the best way to reach and tour the Middle Keys.

Sights

★ Curry Hammock State Park
STATE/PROVINCIAL PARK | FAMILY | On the ocean and bay sides of the Overseas Highway are 260 acres of upland hammock, wetlands, and mangroves. On the bay side, there's a trail through thick hardwoods to a rocky shoreline. The ocean side is more developed, with a sandy beach, a clean bathhouse, picnic tables, a playground, grills, and a 28-site campground with electric and water hookups. Locals consider the paddling trails under canopies of arching mangroves among the best kayaking spots in the Keys. Manatees frequent the area, and it's a great place for watching herons, egrets, ibises, plovers, and sanderlings. Raptors are often seen in the park, too, especially during migration periods. ⊠ *MM 57 OS, 56200 Overseas Hwy., Grassy Key* ☎ *305/289–2690* ⊕ *www.floridastateparks.org/parks-and-trails/*

Spend the day surrounded by nature at Curry Hammock State Park on Grassy Key.

curry-hammock-state-park ✉ *$5 for up to 2 people, $1 per additional person* ☞ *Campsites are $36 per night.*

Dolphin Research Center

OTHER ATTRACTION | FAMILY | The 1963 movie *Flipper* popularized the notion of humans interacting with dolphins, and Milton Santini, the film's creator, opened this center, which is home to a colony of dolphins and sea lions. The nonprofit center has educational sessions and programs that allow you to greet the dolphins from dry land or play with them in their watery habitat. You can even paint a T-shirt with a dolphin—you pick the paint, the dolphin "designs" your shirt. ✉ *MM 59 BS, 58901 Overseas Hwy., Grassy Key* ☎ *305/289–1121 information, 305/289–0002 reservations* ⊕ *www.dolphins.org* ✉ *$28.*

🍽 Restaurants

★ Hideaway Café

$$$ | AMERICAN | It's easy to miss this café tucked between Grassy Key and Marathon, but when you find it (upstairs at Rainbow Bend Resort), expect it to be filled with locals who appreciate a well-planned menu, lovely ocean view, and quiet evening away from the crowds. For starters, dig into escargots à la Edison (sautéed with vegetables, pepper, cognac, and cream) before feasting on specialties, such as a rarely found chateaubriand for one or a seafood medley combining the catch of the day with scallops and shrimp. **Known for:** seclusion and quiet; amazing escargots; hand-cut steaks and fresh fish. $ *Average main: $30* ✉ *Rainbow Bend Resort, MM 58 OS, 57784 Overseas Hwy., Grassy Key* ☎ *305/289–1554* ⊕ *www.hideawaycafe.net* ☺ *No lunch.*

Hotels

★ Grassy Flats

$$ | RESORT | FAMILY | Owned by retired professional kiteboarder Matt Soxton, this relaxed, eco-friendly resort and beach club is popular with water-sports enthusiasts, who make regular visits to its sibling property, The Lagoon, for wakeboarding sessions. **Pros:** peaceful atmosphere; no resort fee; complimentary paddleboards and kayaks. **Cons:** not close to sights in Marathon; Conch House rooms close to highway; limited food options. $ *Rooms from: $299* ✉ *MM 59, 58182 Overseas Hwy., Grassy Key* ☎ *305/998–4590* ⊕ *www.grassyflats.com* ⤳ *33 units* ⏹ *No Meals.*

Gulf View Waterfront Resort

$ | RESORT | This homey duplex on the water is a comfortable, no frills, owner-occupied resort, where the units are individually decorated and have simple wicker furniture and tropical pastels. **Pros:** park-like setting; sandy area with hammocks and tikis; close to restaurants. **Cons:** no elevator to office and second-story accommodations; some traffic noise; not a swimming beach. $ *Rooms from: $182* ✉ *MM 58.7 BS, 58743 Overseas Hwy., Grassy Key* ☎ *305/289–1414, 877/289–0111* ⊕ *www.gulfviewwaterfrontresort. com* ⤳ *11 units* ⏹ *No Meals.*

⚡ Activities

The Lagoon on Grassy Key

WATER SPORTS | FAMILY | This 50-acre, water-sports complex is home to Keys Cable Park, Bongos Beer Garden, and The Lagoon Saloon surf shop. Keys Cable Park specializes in wakeboarding, with additional activities including stand-up paddleboarding, efoil (electric hydrofoil) boarding, and kayaking. Bongos, a locals' favorite venue with live music and a weekend brunch, has a laid-back feel with hammock chairs and lawn games. The Lagoon Saloon, living up to its "Surf, Sail, Swim, and Swill" motto, sells the latest in wind, surf, skate, and lifestyle clothing and accessories and has beer on tap at the register. ✉ *MM 59, 59300 Overseas Hwy., Grassy Key* ☎ *305/414–8245* ⊕ *ridethelagoon. com* ⤳ *$35.*

Marathon

Between MM 53 and 47.5.

New Englanders founded this former fishing village in the early 1800s. The community on Vaca Key subsequently served as a base for pirates, salvagers (also known as "wreckers"), spongers, and, later, Bahamian farmers who eked out a living growing cotton and other crops. More Bahamians arrived in the hope of finding work building the railroad. According to local lore, Marathon was renamed when a worker commented that it was a marathon task to position the tracks across the 6-mile-long island.

During the building of the railroad, Marathon developed a reputation for lawlessness that rivaled that of the Old West. It is said that to keep the rowdy workers from descending on Key West for their off-hours endeavors, residents would send boatloads of liquor up to Marathon. Needless to say, things have quieted down considerably since then.

Still, Marathon is a bustling town, at least compared to other communities in the Keys. As it leaves something to be desired in the charm department, Marathon may not be your first choice of places to stay, but water-sports types will find plenty to enjoy, and its historic and natural attractions merit a visit. Surprisingly good dining options abound, so you'll definitely want to stop for a bite even if you're just passing through on the way to Key West. And the sprawling new Isla Bella Beach Resort has drawn plenty of visitors to Marathon looking for an upscale getaway in the Keys.

Marathon hosts fishing tournaments throughout the year (practically monthly), a huge seafood festival in March, and lighted boat parades around the holidays.

GETTING HERE AND AROUND

SuperShuttle charges $190 per passenger for trips from Miami International Airport to the Upper Keys. To go farther into the Keys, you must book an entire 11-person van, which costs about $300 to Marathon. Reserve trips to the airport 24 hours ahead.

Miami-Dade Transit provides daily bus service from Mile Marker 50 in Marathon to the Florida City Walmart Supercenter on the mainland. The bus stops at major shopping centers as well as on demand anywhere along the route during round trips on the hour from 6 am to 10 pm. The cost is $2 one way, exact change required. The Key West Transit bus runs from Marathon to Key West ($4 one way), with scheduled stops along the way.

VISITOR INFORMATION

CONTACT Greater Marathon Chamber of Commerce and Visitor Center.
⌧ *MM 53.5 BS, 12222 Overseas Hwy., Marathon* ☎ *305/743–5417, 800/262–7284* ⊕ *www.floridakeysmarathon.com.*

Sights

Grassy Key segues into Marathon with only a slight increase in traffic and concentration of commercial establishments. Marathon's roots are anchored in fishing and boating, so look for marinas to find local color, charters, and good restaurants.

At its north end, Key Colony Beach is an old-fashioned island neighborhood worth a visit for its shops and restaurants. Nature lovers shouldn't miss Florida Keys Aquarium Encounters and the attractions on Crane Point.

Other good places to leave the main road are at Sombrero Beach Road (Mile Marker 50), which leads to the beach, and 35th Street (Mile Marker 49), which takes you to a funky little marina and restaurant. U.S. 1 hightails through Hog Key and Knight Key before the big leap over Florida Bay and Hawk Channel via the Seven Mile Bridge.

Crane Point Museum, Nature Center, and Historic Site

HISTORY MUSEUM | FAMILY | Tucked away from the highway behind a stand of trees, Crane Point is part of a 63-acre tract that contains the last-known undisturbed thatch-palm hammock. The facility includes the Museum of Natural History of the Florida Keys, which has displays about local wildlife, a seashell exhibit, and a marine-life display that makes you feel like you're at the bottom of the sea. Kids love the replica 17th-century galleon; the pirate dress-up room; and the re-created Cracker House filled with insects, sea-turtle exhibits, and children's activities. On the 1-mile loop trail, visit the Laura Quinn Wild Bird Center and the remnants of a Bahamian village, site of the restored George Adderly House. It is the oldest surviving example of Bahamian tabby (a concrete-like material created from sand and seashells) construction outside Key West. A boardwalk crosses wetlands, rivers, and mangroves before ending at Adderly Village. From November to Easter, docent-led tours are available. Bring good walking shoes and bug repellent. ⌧ *MM 50.5 BS, 5550 Overseas Hwy., Marathon* ☎ *305/743–9100* ⊕ *www.cranepoint.net* 💲 *$14.95.*

★ Florida Keys Aquarium Encounters

AQUARIUM | FAMILY | This isn't your typical large-city aquarium. It's more hands-on and personal, and it's all outdoors with several tiki huts to house the encounters and provide shade as you

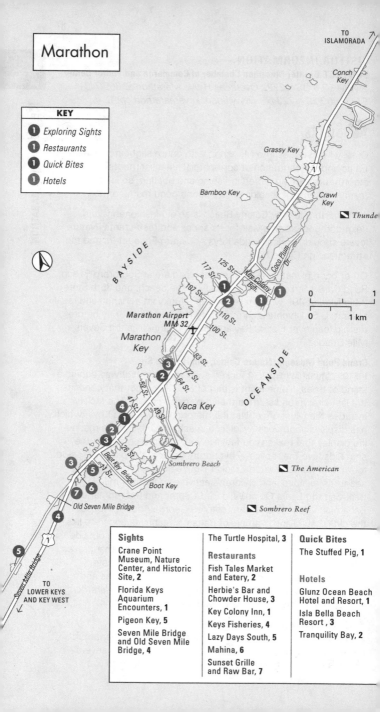

Marathon

KEY
- ① Exploring Sights
- ① Restaurants
- ① Quick Bites
- ① Hotels

TO ISLAMORADA

Conch Key

Grassy Key

Bamboo Key

Crawl Key

Thunde

BAYSIDE

125 St.

117 St.

107 St.

Key Colony Bch.

Coco Plum Dr.

Marathon Airport MM 32

Marathon Key

110 St.

100 St.

83 St.

72 St.

64 St.

49 St.

Vaca Key

OCEANSIDE

52 St.

47 St.

Boot Key Bridge

26 St.

15 St.

Sombrero Beach

Boot Key

The American

Old Seven Mile Bridge

Sombrero Reef

Seven Mile Bridge

TO LOWER KEYS AND KEY WEST

0   1
0   1 km

Sights
Crane Point Museum, Nature Center, and Historic Site, **2**

Florida Keys Aquarium Encounters, **1**

Pigeon Key, **5**

Seven Mile Bridge and Old Seven Mile Bridge, **4**

The Turtle Hospital, **3**

Restaurants
Fish Tales Market and Eatery, **2**

Herbie's Bar and Chowder House, **3**

Key Colony Inn, **1**

Keys Fisheries, **4**

Lazy Days South, **5**

Mahina, **6**

Sunset Grille and Raw Bar, **7**

Quick Bites
The Stuffed Pig, **1**

Hotels
Glunz Ocean Beach Hotel and Resort, **1**

Isla Bella Beach Resort , **3**

Tranquility Bay, **2**

explore, rain or shine. Plan to spend at least two to three hours here. You'll find a 200,000-gallon aquarium and plenty of marine encounters (extra cost), as well as guided tours, viewing areas, and a predator tank. The Coral Reef encounter ($95 snorkel, $130 regulator) lets you dive without hearing the theme from *Jaws* in your head (although you can see several sharks on the other side of the glass). Touch tanks have unique critters like slipper lobsters. Hungry? The on-site Eagle Ray Café serves up wings, fish tacos, salads, burgers, and more. Note that general admission is required, even if you've signed up for a marine encounter ⊠ *MM 53 BS, 11710 Overseas Hwy., Marathon* ☎ *305/407–3262* ⊕ *www. floridakeysaquariumencounters.com* ⊠ *$27.50.*

Pigeon Key

OTHER ATTRACTION | FAMILY | There's much to like about this 5-acre island under the Old Seven Mile Bridge. You might even recognize it from a season finale of the TV show *The Amazing Race.* You can reach it via a restored train that departs from the gift shop, which is in a trailer at Mile Marker 47.5. Once there, tour the island on your own, or join a guided tour to explore the buildings that formed the early-20th-century work camp for the Overseas Railroad, which linked the mainland to Key West in 1912. Later, the island became a fish camp, a state park, and then government-administration headquarters. Exhibits in a small museum recall the history of the Keys, the railroad, and railroad baron Henry M. Flagler. The train ride with tour lasts two hours. ■TIP→ **Bring your own snorkel gear and dive flag and you can snorkel right from the shore; pack a picnic lunch, too.** ⊠ *MM 47.5 BS, 2010 Overseas Hwy., Pigeon Key* ⊹ *Between the Marriott and Hyatt Place* ☎ *305/743–5999* ⊕ *pigeonkey.net* ⊠ *$25.*

★ Seven Mile Bridge and Old Seven Mile Bridge

BRIDGE | FAMILY | This is one of the most photographed images in the Keys. Actually measuring slightly less than 7 miles, it connects the Middle and Lower Keys and is believed to be the world's longest segmental bridge, with 39 expansion joints separating its various concrete sections. Each April, runners gather in Marathon for the annual Seven Mile Bridge Run.

The expanse running parallel to the Seven Mile Bridge is what remains of the Old Seven Mile Bridge, an engineering and architectural marvel in its day that's now on the National Register of Historic Places. Once proclaimed the Eighth Wonder of the World, it rested on a record 546 concrete piers. A $44 million renovation, begun in 2017, is part of a 30-year, $77-million restoration and maintenance agreement between the Keys' Monroe County, Marathon municipal officials, and the Florida Department

Turtle Time

Five species of threatened and endangered sea turtles frequent the waters of the Florida Keys. The **loggerhead,** the most common, is named for the shape of its noggin. It grows to a heft of 300 pounds. It is the only one of the local turtles listed as threatened rather than endangered.

The vegetarian **green turtle** was once hunted for its meat, which has brought populations to their endangered stage. It can reach an impressive 500 pounds.

Named for the shape of its mouth, the **hawksbill turtle** is a relative lightweight at 150 pounds. It prefers rocks and reefs for habitat. The Keys are the only U.S. breeding site for the endangered critter.

The largest reptile alive, the **leatherback turtle** can weigh in at up to 2,000 pounds, attained from a diet of mainly jellyfish.

The rarest of local sea turtles, the **Kemp's ridley** is named after a Key West fisherman. A carnivore, it grows to 100 pounds.

The biggest threats to sea turtle survival include fibropapilloma tumors, monofilament fishing lines (which can sever their flippers), entanglement in ropes and nets, boat propeller run-ins, swallowing plastic bags (which appear to them as jellyfish), oil spills, and other human and natural impact.

of Transportation. No cars are allowed on the old bridge, but the oft-photographed, 2.2-mile span is open to pedestrians and serves as the gateway to historic Pigeon Key, an islet nestled beneath the "Old Seven" that was once home to about 400 workers constructing the railroad. ✉ *Marathon.*

The Turtle Hospital
WILDLIFE REFUGE | **FAMILY** | Each year, more than 100 injured creatures are admitted to the world's first state-certified veterinary hospital for sea turtles. Guided 90-minute tours take you into recovery and surgical areas. In the "hospital bed" tanks, you can see recovering patients and others that are permanent residents due to their injuries. After the tour, you can feed some of the residents. Call ahead—space is limited and tours are sometimes canceled due to medical emergencies. The turtle ambulance out front makes for a memorable souvenir photo. ✉ *MM 48.5 BS, 2396 Overseas Hwy., Marathon* ☎ *305/743–2552* ⊕ *www.turtle-hospital.org* 🎟 *$30.*

Driving along the Seven Mile Bridge, which connects the Middle and Lower Keys, is one of the great thrills of a visit to the Keys.

Beaches

★ Sombrero Beach

BEACH | FAMILY | One of the best beaches in the Keys has shaded picnic areas overlooking a coconut palm–lined grassy stretch and the Atlantic. Roped-off areas allow swimmers, boaters, and windsurfers to share the narrow cove. Facilities include grills, a large playground, a pier, a volleyball court, and a paved, lighted bike path off the Overseas Highway. Sunday afternoons draw lots of local families toting coolers. The park is accessible for those with disabilities and allows leashed pets. Turn east at the traffic light in Marathon and follow signs to the end. **Amenities:** showers; toilets. **Best for:** swimming; windsurfing. ⊠ *MM 50 OS, Sombrero Beach Rd., Marathon* ☎ *305/743–0033* 🎫 *Free.*

Restaurants

Fish Tales Market and Eatery

$ | SEAFOOD | This no-frills, roadside eatery has a loyal local following, an unfussy ambience, a couple of outside picnic tables, and friendly service. Signature dishes include snapper on grilled rye with coleslaw and melted Muenster cheese, a fried-fish burrito, George's crab cake, and tomato-based conch chowder. **Known for:** luscious lobster bisque; fresh and affordable seafood and meat market; affordable specials. ⑤ *Average main: $14* ⊠ *MM 52.5 OS, 11711 Overseas Hwy., Marathon* ☎ *305/743–9196, 888/662–4822* ⊕ *www.floridalobster.com* ⊗ *Closed weekends.*

Herbie's Bar and Chowder House

$ | SEAFOOD | This shack-like spot has been the go-to for quick, affordable comfort food since the 1940s. You'll find all the Old Keys staples—conch, lobster tail, fried oysters, and fresh fish— as well as cheeseburgers and filet mignon. **Known for:** great craft-beer selection; crispy conch fritters; good key lime pie. ⑤ *Average main: $14 ⊠ MM 50.5, 6350 Overseas Hwy., Marathon ☎ 305/743–6373 ⊕ www.herbiesrestaurant.com ⊙ Closed Sun.–Tues.*

Key Colony Inn

$$ | ITALIAN | The inviting aroma of an Italian kitchen pervades this family-owned favorite. For lunch there are fish and steak entrées served with fries, salad, and bread in addition to Italian specialties; dinner features veal Oscar and other traditional dishes, as well as specialties like seafood *taliano,* a dish of scallops and shrimp sautéed in garlic butter and served with marinara sauce over linguine. **Known for:** friendly and attentive service; Italian specialties; Sunday brunch (November through April). ⑤ *Average main: $20 ⊠ MM 54 OS, 700 W. Ocean Dr., Marathon ☎ 305/743–0100 ⊕ www.kcinn. com.*

Keys Fisheries

$ | SEAFOOD | FAMILY | You can't miss the enormous tiki bar on stilts, but the walk-up window on the ground floor is the heart of this warehouse-turned-restaurant. The huge lobster Reuben served on thick slices of toasted bread is the signature dish, and the adults-only upstairs tiki bar offers a sushi and raw bar for eat-in only. **Known for:** seafood market; marina views; fish-food dispensers (25¢) so you can feed the tarpon. ⑤ *Average main: $16 ⊠ MM 49 BS, 3390 Gulfview Ave., at the end of 35th St., Marathon ⊹ Turn onto 35th St. from Overseas Hwy. ☎ 305/743–4353, 866/743–4353 ⊕ www.keysfisheries.com.*

Lazy Days South

$$ | SEAFOOD | Tucked into Marathon Marina, ½ mile north of the Seven Mile Bridge, this restaurant offers views just as spectacular as its highly lauded food. The offerings at this spinoff of an Islamorada favorite range from fried or sautéed conch and a coconut-fried fish du jour sandwich to seafood pastas and beef tips over rice. **Known for:** water views; delicious seafood entrées; hook and cook. ⑤ *Average main: $22 ⊠ MM 47.3 OS, 725 11th St., Marathon ☎ 305/289–0839 ⊕ www.lazydayssouth.com.*

★ Mahina

$$ | ITALIAN | Dishes such as ahi poke and lobster-crusted mahimahi nod to executive chef Pavy Keomaniboth's native Hawaii. The spectacular indoor–outdoor setting features coconut palms strung with lights and panoramic sunset views. **Known for:** Hawaiian-inspired dishes and cocktails; romantic; extensive wine list. $ *Average main: $24 ⊠ Isla Bella Resort, MM 47 OS, 1 Knights Key Blvd., Marathon ☎ 786/638–8106 ⊕ www.islabellabeachresort. com.*

Sunset Grille and Raw Bar

$$ | SEAFOOD | Treat yourself to a seafood lunch or dinner at this vaulted tiki hut at the foot of the Seven Mile Bridge. For lunch, try the Voodoo grouper sandwich topped with mango-guava mayo (and wear your swimsuit if you want to take a dip in the pool afterward); dinner specialties include a Brie-stuffed filet mignon and coconut curry lobster. **Known for:** weekend pool parties and barbecues; pricey dinner specials; a swimming pool for patrons. $ *Average main: $24 ⊠ MM 47 OS, 7 Knights Key Blvd., Marathon ☎ 305/396–7235 ⊕ www.sunsetgrille7milebridge.com.*

Coffee and Quick Bites

The Stuffed Pig

$ | AMERICAN | With only nine tables and a counter inside, this place is always full. The kitchen whips up daily lunch specials like seafood platters or pulled pork with hand-cut fries, but the all-day breakfast is the main draw. **Known for:** local twists on breakfast standards; large portions; cash only. $ *Average main: $11 ⊠ MM 49 BS, 3520 Overseas Hwy., Marathon ☎ 305/743–4059 ⊕ www. thestuffedpig.com* ▤ *No credit cards* ⊙ *No dinner.*

🛏 Hotels

Glunz Ocean Beach Hotel and Resort

$$ | HOTEL | The Glunz family got it right when they purchased this former time-share property and put a whole lot of love into ensuring it achieved its full oceanfront potential—from the bottom-floor rooms, you can walk out your back door and your feet are in the sand, or you can also chill at the oceanfront tiki bar or one of two heated pools. **Pros:** friendly staff; nice private beach; excellent free Wi-Fi. **Cons:** small elevator; no interior corridors; not cheap. $ *Rooms from: $300 ⊠ MM 53.5 OS, 351 E. Ocean Dr., Marathon ☎ 305/289–0525 ⊕ www.glunzoceanbeachhotel.com* ⇆ *46 units* ⚏ *No Meals.*

★ Isla Bella Beach Resort

$$ | RESORT | FAMILY | Combining Caribbean luxury with Keys charm, this glamorous 24-acre resort is a destination unto itself with five pools, rooms along a sandy waterfront, toes-in-the-sand dining, and amenities like kids activities, resort bikes, and morning yoga.

One of the most popular beaches in the Keys is Marathon's white-sand Sombrero Beach.

Pros: secluded setting; spacious rooms; full-service spa and marina. **Cons:** no real beach; a hefty resort fee; some balconies lack privacy. $ *Rooms from: $250* ⊠ *MM 47 OS, 1 Knights Key Blvd., Marathon* ☎ *305/481–9451* ⊕ *www.islabellabeachresort.com* ⇰ *199 rooms* ⚭ *No Meals.*

★ Tranquility Bay

$$$$ | RESORT | FAMILY | Ralph Lauren could have designed the rooms at this stylish, luxurious resort on a nice beach. **Pros:** secluded setting; tiki bar on the beach; main pool is nice and big. **Cons:** a bit sterile; no privacy on balconies; cramped building layout. $ *Rooms from: $425* ⊠ *MM 48.5 BS, 2600 Overseas Hwy., Marathon* ☎ *305/289–0888, 866/643–5397* ⊕ *www.tranquilitybay.com* ⇰ *102 rooms* ⚭ *No Meals.*

Activities

BIKING

Tooling around on two wheels is a good way to see Marathon. There's easy cycling on a 1-mile off-road path that connects to the 2 miles of the Old Seven Mile Bridge leading to Pigeon Key.

Bike Marathon Bike Rental

BIKING | "Have bikes, will deliver" could be the motto of this company, which will transport beach cruisers (as well as helmets, baskets, and locks) to your hotel door. It also rents kayaks. There's no physical location, but services are available Monday through

Saturday 9–4 and Sunday 9–2. ✉ *Marathon* ☎ *305/743–3204* ⊕ *www.bikemarathonbikerentals.com* 💲 *$69 per wk.*

BOATING

Sail, motor, or paddle: boating is what the Keys are all about. Brave the Atlantic waves and reefs, or explore backcountry islands on the gulf side. If you don't have a lot of boating and chart-reading experience, tap into local knowledge on a charter.

Captain Pip's

BOATING | This operator rents 18- to 24-foot outboards as well as snorkeling gear. Ask about multiday deals, or try one of the accommodation packages and walk right from your bay-front room to your boat. ✉ *MM 47.5 BS, 1410 Overseas Hwy., Marathon* ☎ *305/743–4403, 800/707–1692* ⊕ *www.captainpips.com* 💲 *Rentals from $199 per day.*

FISHING

For recreational anglers, the deepwater fishing is superb in both the bay and the ocean. Marathon Hump (West Hump), one good spot, has depths ranging from 500 to more than 1,000 feet. Locals fish from a half dozen bridges, including Long Key Bridge, the Old Seven Mile Bridge, and both ends of Tom's Harbor. Barracuda, bonefish, and tarpon all frequent local waters.

Marathon Lady

FISHING | Morning, afternoon, and night, fish for mahimahi, grouper, and other tasty catches aboard this 73-footer, which departs on half-day excursions from the Vaca Cut Bridge (Mile Marker 53), north of Marathon. Join the crew for night fishing ($55) from 6:30 to midnight from Memorial Day to Labor Day. ✉ *MM 53 OS, 11711 Overseas Hwy., at 117th St., Marathon* ☎ *305/743–5580* ⊕ *www.marathonlady.net* 💲 *From $45.*

Sea Dog Charters

FISHING | Captain Jim Purcell, a deep-sea specialist for ESPN's *The American Outdoorsman,* provides one of the best values in Keys fishing. His company offers half- and full-day offshore, reef and wreck, and backcountry fishing trips, as well as fishing and snorkeling trips aboard 30- to 37-foot boats. The per-person cost for a half-day trip is the same regardless of whether or not your group fills the boat, and it includes bait, light tackle, ice, coolers, and fishing licenses. If you prefer an all-day private charter on a 37-foot boat, he offers those, too, for up to six people. A fuel surcharge may apply. ✉ *MM 47.5 BS, 1248 Overseas Hwy., Marathon* ☎ *305/743–8255* ⊕ *www.seadogcharters.net* 💲 *From $60.*

GOLF

Key Colony Beach Golf & Tennis

GOLF | Designed by Wayne Spano and opened in 1973, this 9-holer near Marathon has no reserved tee times, and there's never a rush to hurry up and play through. In fact, you can finish in about 45 minutes even with slow greens as it's an easy, flat course to walk. Just show up any time from 7:30 am to dusk. Regulars say you only need three clubs to play the entire course, making it perfect for beginners or those who can't hit far. A little pro shop meets basic golf needs. Club rentals are only $3 per person, but the choices are a bit worn; pull carts are $2. You'll also have free use of the club's lighted tennis courts. ⊠ *MM 53.5 OS, 460 8th St., Marathon* ☎ *305/289–9859* 🖅 *$13 for 9 holes, $8 for each additional 9 holes* 🏌 *9 holes, 972 yards, par 3.*

SCUBA DIVING AND SNORKELING

Many dive operators head to Sombrero Reef and Lighthouse, the most popular down-under destination in these parts; some also go to Looe Key Reef. For a shallow dive and some lobster nabbing, Coffins Patch, off Key Colony Beach, is good, and wrecks like the *Thunderbolt* serve as artificial reefs.

Spirit Snorkeling

SNORKELING | **FAMILY** | Join regularly scheduled snorkeling excursions to Sombrero Reef and its Lighthouse on this company's comfortable catamaran. It also offers sunset cruises and private charters. ⊠ *MM 47.5 BS, 1410 Overseas Hwy., Slip No. 1, Marathon* ☎ *305/289–0614* ⊕ *www.captainpips.com* 🖅 *From $49.*

Tilden's Scuba Center

SCUBA DIVING | Since the mid-1980s, Tilden's Scuba Center has been providing lessons, gear rental, and snorkel, scuba, and Snuba adventures. Look for the huge, colorful angelfish sculpture outside the building. ⊠ *MM 49.5 BS, 4650 Overseas Hwy., Marathon* ☎ *305/743–7255, 888/728–2235* ⊕ *www.tildensscubacenter.com* 🖅 *From $60 for snorkel trips; from $70 for dive trips.*

THE LOWER KEYS

Updated by
Sara Liss

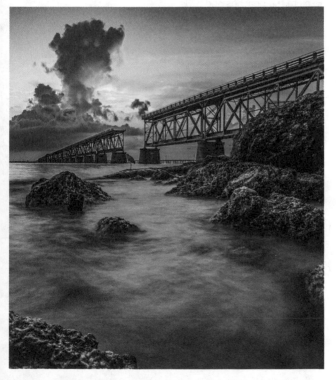

⊙ Sights   🍴 Restaurants   🛏 Hotels   ● Shopping   🍸 Nightlife

★★★☆☆   ★★★★☆   ★★★★☆   ★★★☆☆   ★★★☆☆

WELCOME TO THE LOWER KEYS

TOP REASONS TO GO

★ **Wildlife viewing:** The Lower Keys are populated with all kinds of animals. Watch especially for the Key deer but also other wildlife at Blue Hole in the National Key Deer Refuge.

★ **Bahia Honda State Park:** Explore the beaches and trails, and then camp for the night at this gorgeous state park.

★ **Kayaking:** Get out in a kayak to spot birds in the Keys' backcountry wildlife refuges.

★ **Snorkeling:** Grab a mask and fins and head to Looe Key Reef to see amazing coral formations and fish so bright and animated they look like cartoons.

★ **Fishing:** A full range of fishing is great in the Lower Keys. Cast from a bridge, boat, or shoreline flats for bonefish, tarpon, and other feisty catches.

1 Bahia Honda Key. Bahia Honda State Park is the main attraction on this small island in the Lower Keys. The 524-acre park, which takes up both sides of the Overseas Highway, is blessed with a sandy coastline boasting several beaches, including the beautiful mile-long Sandspur Beach.

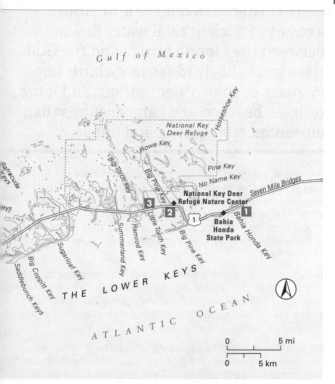

Gulf of Mexico

National Key Deer Refuge

Horseshoe Key

Howe Key

Pine Key

No Name Key

Barracuda Keys

Big Torch Key

Big Pine Key

Seven Mile Bridges

National Key Deer Refuge Nature Center

Little Torch Key

Ramrod Key

Summerland Key

Big Pine Key

Bahia Honda State Park

Bahia Honda Key

Sugarloaf Key

Big Coppitt Key

Saddlebunch Keys

THE LOWER KEYS

ATLANTIC OCEAN

0 — 5 mi
0 — 5 km

2 Big Pine Key. Wildlife abounds on Big Pine Key, especially at the massive National Key Deer Refuge, which was founded in 1957 to protect the dwindling population of Key deer. Fishing, biking, and kayaking through mangrove islands are all popular pastimes.

3 Little Torch Key. Little Torch is just a 40-minute drive from Key West, and many opt to stay in this quieter area and venture into Key West for day trips. There are plenty of water sports to keep you busy, as well as exclusive Little Palm Island Resort, located on its own private island.

Beginning at Bahia Honda Key, the islands of the Florida Keys become smaller, more clustered, and more numerous, a result of ancient tidal water flowing between the Florida Straits and the Gulf. Here you're likely to see more birds and mangroves than other tourists, and more refuges, beaches, and campgrounds than museums, restaurants, and hotels.

The islands are made up of two types of limestone, both denser than the highly permeable Key Largo limestone of the Upper Keys. As a result, fresh water forms in pools rather than percolating through the rock, creating watering holes that support alligators, snakes, deer, rabbits, raccoons, and migratory ducks. (Many of these animals can be seen in the National Key Deer Refuge on Big Pine Key.)

The Lower Keys also have both Looe Key Reef, arguably the Keys' most beautiful tract of coral, and Bahia Honda State Park, home to what is considered one of the world's best beaches owing to its fine sand dunes; clear, warm water; and panoramic vista of bridges, hammocks, and azure sky and sea.

Big Pine Key is fishing headquarters for a laid-back community that swells with retirees in the winter. South of it, the dribble of keys includes Little Torch, Middle Torch, Ramrod, Summerland, Cudjoe, Sugarloaf, and Saddlebunch. They can flash by in a blink of an eye if you don't take the time to stop at a roadside eatery or check out tours and charters at the little marinas.

Just off Little Torch Key, Little Palm Island once welcomed U.S. presidents and other notables to its secluded fishing camp. It was also the location for the movie *PT 109* about John F. Kennedy's celebrated World War II heroism. Today it still offers respite to the upper class in the form of an exclusive getaway resort accessible only by boat or seaplane.

Planning

Getting Oriented

In truth, the Lower Keys include Key West, but since it's as different from the rest of the Lower Keys as peanut butter is from jelly, this section covers just the keys between Mile Marker 38.5 and Mile Marker 9. The Seven Mile Bridge drops you into the lap of this homey, quiet area.

Heed speed limits in these parts. They may seem incredibly strict, given that the traffic is the lightest of anywhere in the Keys, but the purpose is to protect the resident Key deer population, and officers of the law pay close attention.

Getting Here and Around

To get to the Lower Keys, fly into either Miami International Airport or Key West International Airport. Key West is considerably closer, but it has far fewer flights. Rental cars are available at both airports, and there's bus service from the Key West airport ($4 one way) with Key West Transit.

Hotels

Fishing lodges, dive resorts, and campgrounds are the most prevalent type of lodging in this part of the Keys. Rates are generally much lower than on other Keys, especially Key West, which makes this a good place to stay if you're on a budget.

Restaurants

Restaurants are few and far between in the Lower Keys, and they mostly consist of seafood joints where dinner is fresh off the hook and license plates or dollar bills stuck to the wall count for decor. For a special occasion, hop aboard the ferry at Little Torch Key to experience the globe-trotting cuisine of private Little Palm Island Resort & Spa. Restaurants may close for two to four weeks during the slow season (mid-September to mid-November).

Hotel and restaurant reviews have been shortened. For full information, visit Fodors.com. Hotel prices are the lowest cost of a standard double room in high season. Restaurant prices are the average cost of a main course at dinner or, if dinner is not served, at lunch.

What It Costs			
$	$$	$$$	$$$$
RESTAURANTS			
under $20	$20–$25	$26–$35	over $35
HOTELS			
under $200	$200–$300	$301–$400	Over $400

Bahia Honda Key

Between MM 38.5 and 36.

All of Bahia Honda Key is devoted to its eponymous state park, which keeps it in a pristine state. Besides the park's outdoor activities, it offers an up-close view of the original railroad bridge.

GETTING HERE AND AROUND

Bahia Honda Key is near the southern terminus of the Seven Mile Bridge. A two-lane road travels its 2-mile length. It is 32 miles north of Key West and served by Key West Transit buses.

Sights

★ Bahia Honda State Park

STATE/PROVINCIAL PARK | FAMILY | Most first-time visitors to the region are dismayed by the lack of beaches—but then they discover Bahia Honda Key. The 524-acre park sprawls across both sides of the highway, giving it 2½ miles of fabulous sandy coastline. Beaches include Sandspur and Loggerhead Beaches on the Atlantic side and Calusa Beach, which faces the Gulf of Mexico. The snorkeling isn't bad, either; there's underwater life (soft coral, queen conchs, random little fish) just a few hundred feet offshore. Seasonal ranger-led nature programs take place at or depart from the Sand and Sea Nature Center. There are rental cabins and a campground, snack bar, gift shop, and 19-slip marina, as well as facilities for renting kayaks and arranging snorkeling tours. Get a panoramic view of the island from what's left of the railroad—the Bahia Honda Rail Bridge. ⊠ *MM 37 OS, 36850 Overseas Hwy., Bahia Honda Key* ☎ *305/872–2353* ⊕ *www.floridastateparks.org/park/Bahia-Honda* 🎫 *From $5.*

A tropical beach vista at Bahia Honda State Park on Bahia Honda Key

🏊 Beaches

Calusa Beach

BEACH | FAMILY | Located at the southernmost point of Bahia Honda State Park, this public beach is a calm and pleasant spot for sunbathing, swimming, and snorkeling. It's shallow enough for little ones to wade in, and the sand is velvety soft and clean (as opposed to some of the rockier beaches in Key West). There are public restrooms and showers nearby. Camping sites are available, but they tend to book up, so reservations are recommended in high season. **Amenities:** parking (no fee); showers; toilets; water sports. **Best for:** swimming; walking. ✉ *MM 37 OS, 36850 Overseas Hwy., Bahia Honda Key* ☎ *305/872–2353* ⊕ *www.floridastateparks.org/park/Bahia-Honda* 🎫 *From $5.*

Loggerhead Beach

BEACH | FAMILY | What is sometimes called "the Oceanside Beach" offers an excellent view of Henry Flagler's old railroad bridge. A small rock island not far from shore is easy enough to kayak around (rentals are available elsewhere in Bahia Honda State Park), and there are plenty of snorkeling opportunities in the clear waters. This beach doesn't have picnic pavilions, and its comparative lack of amenities makes it less crowded and more rustic than other park beaches. **Amenities:** parking (no fee). **Best for:** solitude; swimming, walking. ✉ *MM 37 OS, 36850 Overseas Hwy., Bahia Honda Key* ☎ *305/872–2353* ⊕ *www.floridastateparks.org/park/Bahia-Honda* 🎫 *From $5.*

★ Sandspur Beach

BEACH | FAMILY | Of Bahia Honda State Park's three beaches, which also include Calusa and Loggerhead, Sandspur is the largest. It's also regularly declared the best beach in the Florida Keys, and you'll be hard pressed to argue. The sand is baby-powder soft, and the aqua water is warm, clear, and shallow. Mild currents here and at the other beaches make them great for swimming, even with small fry. **Amenities:** food and drink; parking (no fee); showers; toilets; water sports. **Best for:** snorkeling; swimming. ⊠ *MM 37 OS, 36850 Overseas Hwy., Bahia Honda Key* ☎ *305/872–2353* ⊕ *www.floridastateparks.org/park/Bahia-Honda* 🎫 *From $5.*

Hotels

Bahia Honda State Park Cabins

$ | HOTEL | Elsewhere you'd pay big bucks for the wonderful views available at these three cabins, each of which has two two-bedroom units with full kitchens and baths, as well as air-conditioning (but no television, radio, or phone). **Pros:** great Florida Bay views; beachfront camping; affordable rates. **Cons:** books up fast; area can be buggy; need to bring toiletries. ⑤ *Rooms from: $163* ⊠ *MM 37 OS, 36850 Overseas Hwy., Bahia Honda Key* ☎ *305/872–2353, 800/326–3521* ⊕ *www.reserveamerica.com* 🛏 *6 cabins* ⧉ *No Meals.*

Activities

SCUBA DIVING AND SNORKELING
Bahia Honda Dive Shop

SNORKELING | FAMILY | The concessionaire at Bahia Honda State Park manages a 19-slip marina; rents wet suits, snorkel equipment, and corrective masks; and operates twice-daily off-shore-reef snorkel trips. You can also rent kayaks and beach chairs here. ⊠ *MM 37 OS, 36850 Overseas Hwy., Bahia Honda Key* ☎ *305/872–3210* ⊕ *www.bahiahondapark.com* ⌇ *Kayak rentals from $10 per hr; snorkel tours from $30.*

Big Pine Key

Between MM 32–30.

Welcome to the Keys' most natural holdout, where wildlife refuges protect rare and endangered animals. Here you swap the commercialism of the Upper Keys for an authentic backcountry atmosphere. How could things get more casual than Key Largo, you might wonder? Find out by exiting U.S. 1 to explore the habitat of the charmingly diminutive Key deer or cast a line from No Name Key Bridge.

Tours explore the expansive waters of the National Key Deer Refuge and Great White Heron National Wildlife Refuge, one of the first such refuges in the country. Along with Key West National Wildlife Refuge, it encompasses more than 200,000 acres of water and more than 8,000 acres of land on 49 small islands. Besides its namesake bird, Great White Heron National Wildlife Refuge provides habitat for uncounted species of birds and three species of sea turtles. It is the only U.S. breeding site for the endangered hawksbill turtle.

GETTING HERE AND AROUND

Most people rent a car to get to Big Pine Key so they can also explore Key West and other parts of the chain.

VISITOR INFORMATION

CONTACT Lower Keys Chamber of Commerce. ⊠ *31020 Overseas Hwy., Big Pine Key* ☎ *305/872–2411, 800/872–3722* ⊕ *www.lowerkeyschamber.com.*

Sights

National Key Deer Refuge

WILDLIFE REFUGE | FAMILY | This 84,824-acre refuge was established in 1957 to protect the dwindling population of the Key deer, one of more than 22 animals and plants federally classified as endangered or threatened. The Key deer, which stands about 30 inches at the shoulders and is a subspecies of the Virginia white-tailed deer, once roamed throughout the Lower and Middle Keys, but hunting, destruction of their habitat, and a growing human population caused their numbers to decline to 27 by the middle of the last century. The deer have made a comeback, increasing their numbers to approximately 750. The best place to see them in the refuge is at the end of Key Deer Boulevard and on No Name Key, a sparsely populated island just east of Big Pine Key. Mornings and evenings are the best time to spot them. Deer may turn up along the road at any time of day, so drive slowly. They wander into nearby yards to nibble tender grass and bougainvillea blossoms, but locals do not appreciate tourists driving into their neighborhoods after them. Feeding them is against the law and puts them in danger.

A quarry left over from railroad days, Blue Hole is the largest body of fresh water in the Keys. From the observation platform and nearby walking trail, you might see the resident alligators, turtles,

Head to the National Key Deer Refuge on Big Pine Key to see endangered Key deer.

and other wildlife. There are two well-marked trails, recently revamped: the Jack Watson Nature Trail (0.6 miles), named after an environmentalist and the refuge's first warden, and the Fred C. Mannillo Wildlife Trail (0.2 miles), one of the most wheelchair-accessible places to see an unspoiled pine-rockland forest and wetlands. The visitor center has exhibits on Keys biology and ecology. The refuge also provides information on Key West National Wildlife Refuge and Great White Heron National Wildlife Refuge. Accessible only by water, both are popular with kayak outfitters. ⊠ *Visitor Center–Headquarters, Big Pine Shopping Center, MM 30.5 BS, 28950 Watson Blvd., Big Pine Key* ☎ *305/872–2239* ⊕ *www.fws. gov/nationalkeydeer* ✆ *Free* ⊙ *Visitor center closed Sun. and Mon.*

🍴 Restaurants

No Name Pub

$ | **AMERICAN** | This honky-tonk has been around since 1936, delighting the inveterate locals and the intrepid vacationers who come for the excellent pizza, cold beer, and *interesting* companionship. The decor, such as it is, amounts to the autographed dollar bills that cover every inch of the place. **Known for:** shrimp pizza and fish sandwich; fried grouper sandwiches; conch chowder. ⑤ *Average main: $15* ⊠ *MM 30 BS, 30813 Watson Blvd., Big Pine Key* ✥ *From U.S. 1, turn west on Wilder Rd., left on South St., right on Ave. B, right on Watson Blvd.* ☎ *305/872–9115* ⊕ *www. nonamepub.com.*

Coffee and Quick Bites

Good Food Conspiracy

$ | **VEGETARIAN** | Like a fine wine, this small natural-foods eatery and market surrenders its pleasures a little at a time. Step inside to the aroma of brewing coffee, and then pick up the scent of fresh strawberries or carrots being blended into a smoothie and the green aroma of wheatgrass juice, followed by the earthy odor of hummus. **Known for:** vegetarian and vegan dishes; sandwiches and smoothies; organic items. **$** *Average main: $10* ⊠ *MM 30.2 OS, 30150 Overseas Hwy., Big Pine Key* ☎ *305/872–3945* ⊕ *www. goodfoodconspiracy.com* ⊗ *No dinner Sun.*

🛏 Hotels

Big Pine Key Resort

$ | **HOTEL** | **FAMILY** | There's a congenial atmosphere at this lively, family-owned lodge-campground-marina—a happy mix of tent campers (who have the fabulous waterfront real estate), RVers (who look pretty permanent), and motel dwellers who like to mingle at the rooftop pool and play poker. **Pros:** local fishing crowd; nice pool; great price. **Cons:** RV park is too close to motel; deer will eat your food if you're camping; some rooms could use updating. **$** *Rooms from: $159* ⊠ *MM 33 OS, 33000 Overseas Hwy., Big Pine Key* ☎ *305/872–2351* ⊕ *www.covecommunities.com/ rv-resorts/florida/big-pine-key-resort* ⇥ *16 rooms* ⦿ *No Meals* ☞ *To protect Key deer, no dogs allowed.*

Deer Run on the Atlantic

$$ | **B&B/INN** | Wildlife, including the endangered Key deer, roams the grounds of this bed-and-breakfast, which has four guest rooms, all with ocean views, cathedral ceilings, king beds, private baths, small porches, and calming decor. **Pros:** quiet neighborhood; vegan, organic breakfasts; free state park pass and use of bikes, kayaks, and beach towels. **Cons:** no children or pets allowed; a little hard to find; may be too secluded for some. **$** *Rooms from: $200* ⊠ *MM 33 OS, 1997 Long Beach Dr., Big Pine Key* ☎ *305/872–2015* ⊕ *www.deerrunfloridabb.com* ⇥ *4 rooms* ⦿ *Free Breakfast.*

Activities

BIKING

A good 10 miles of paved roads run from Mile Marker 30.3 bay side, along Wilder Road, across the bridge to No Name Key, and along Key Deer Boulevard into the National Key Deer Refuge. On the way you might see some Key deer. Stay off the trails that lead into wetlands, where fat tires can damage the environment.

Big Pine Bicycle Center

BIKING | FAMILY | Owner Marty Baird is an avid cyclist who enjoys sharing his knowledge of great places to ride. He's also skilled at selecting the right bike for the journey, and he knows his repairs, too. His old-fashioned, single-speed, fat-tire cruisers rent by the half or full day. Helmets, baskets, and locks are included. ⊠ *MM 30.9 BS, 31 County Rd., Big Pine Key* ☎ *305/872–0130* ⊕ *www. facebook.com/bigpinebikes* 🖭 *From $25.*

FISHING

Cast from No Name Key Bridge or hire a charter to take you into backcountry or deep waters for fishing year-round.

Captain Hook's Big Pine Key

BOATING | FAMILY | Glass-bottom-boat excursions venture into the backcountry and out onto the Atlantic Ocean. The five-hour Out Island Excursion and Picnic emphasizes nature and Keys history; in addition to close encounters with birds, sea life, and vegetation, there's a fish cookout on an island. Snorkel and fishing equipment, food, and drinks are included. This is one of the few nature outings in the Keys with wheelchair access. Deep-sea charter rates for up to six people can be arranged for a half or full day. The outfitter also offers flats fishing in the Gulf of Mexico. Dive excursions head to the wreck of the 110-foot *Adolphus Busch Sr.,* and scuba and snorkel trips to Looe Key Reef, prime scuba and snorkeling territory, aboard glass-bottom boats. ⊠ *MM 29.6 BS, 29675 Overseas Hwy., Big Pine Key* ☎ *305/872–9863, 800/654–9560* ⊕ *www. captainhooks.com* 🖭 *From $38.*

KAYAKING

There's nothing like the vast expanse of pristine waters and mangrove islands preserved by national refuges from here to Key West. The mazelike terrain can be confusing, so it's wise to hire a guide at least the first time out.

Big Pine Kayak Adventures

KAYAKING | FAMILY | There's no excuse to skip a water adventure with this convenient kayak rental service, which delivers them to your lodging or anywhere between the Seven Mile Bridge and Stock Island. The company, headed by *The Florida Keys Paddling Guide* author, Bill Keogh, will rent you a kayak and then ferry you—called taxi-yakking—to remote islands with clear instructions on how to paddle back on your own. Rentals are by the half day or full day. Three-hour group kayak tours, which are the cheapest option, explore the mangrove forests of the Key Deer and Great White

Heron National Wildlife Refuges. More expensive four-hour custom tours transport you to exquisite backcountry areas teeming with wildlife. Kayak fishing charters are also popular. Paddleboard ecotours, rentals, and yoga are also available. ⊠ *Old Wooden Bridge Fishing Camp, 1791 Bogie Dr., Big Pine Key ✦ From MM 30, turn right at traffic light, continue on Wilder Rd. toward No Name Key; the fishing camp is just before the bridge with a big yellow kayak on the sign out front* ☎ *305/872–7474* ⊕ *www. keyskayaktours.com* ☞ *From $50.*

SCUBA DIVING AND SNORKELING

Close to Looe Key Reef, this is prime scuba diving and snorkeling territory. Some resorts cater to divers with dive boats that depart from their own dock. Others can make arrangements for you.

Little Torch Key

Between MM 29 and 10.

Little Torch Key and its neighbor islands, Ramrod Key and Summerland Key, are good jumping-off points for divers headed for Looe Key Reef. The islands also serve as a refuge for those who want to make forays into Key West but not stay in the thick of things. Sugarloaf Key and Cudjoe Key have a few dining spots.

The undeveloped backcountry at your door makes Little Torch Key an ideal location for fishing and kayaking. Nearby Ramrod Key, which also caters to divers bound for Looe Key, derives its name from a ship that wrecked on nearby reefs in the early 1800s.

🍴 Restaurants

★ The Dining Room at Little Palm Island Resort

$$$$ | ECLECTIC | The restaurant at the exclusive Little Palm Island Resort—its dining room and adjacent outdoor terrace lit by candles and warmed by live music—is one of the most romantic spots in the Keys. It's open to nonguests on a reservations-only basis, but no one under 16 is allowed on the island. **Known for:** oceanfront tables in the sand; Key deer meandering by your table; Latin and Caribbean flavors. ⑤ *Average main: $65* ⊠ *MM 28.5 OS, 28500 Overseas Hwy., Little Torch Key* ☎ *305/872–2551* ⊕ *www. littlepalmisland.com.*

The Fish Camp at Geiger Key Marina

$ | AMERICAN | There's a strong hint of the Old Keys at this oceanside marina restaurant, where local fishermen stop for breakfast before heading out to catch the big one, and everyone shows up on Sunday for the barbecue from 4 to 9. "On the backside of paradise," as the sign says, its tiki structures overlook quiet mangroves at an RV park marina. Locals usually outnumber tourists. **Known for:** local hangout; casual atmosphere on the water; conch fritters loaded with conch. $ *Average main: $16* ⊠ *MM 10, 5 Geiger Key Rd., off Boca Chica Rd., Geiger Key* ☎ *305/296–3553, 305/294–1230* ⊕ *www.geigerkeymarina.com.*

Mangrove Mama's

$$ | SEAFOOD | FAMILY | This could be the prototype for a Keys restaurant, given its shanty appearance, lattice trim, and roving sort of indoor-outdoor floor plan. Then there's the seafood, from the ubiquitous fish sandwich (fried, grilled, broiled, or blackened) to the lobster Reubens, crab cakes, and coconut shrimp. **Known for:** pizza; award-winning conch chowder; slow service. $ *Average main: $20* ⊠ *MM 20 BS, 19991 Overseas Hwy., Sugarloaf Key* ☎ *305/745–3030* ⊕ *www.mangrovemamasrestaurant.com.*

★ My New Joint

$ | AMERICAN | Atop the famed Square Grouper restaurant is a secret spot that locals love and smart travelers seek out for its tapas and well-stocked bar. Sit at a high-top table or on a sofa, and savor made-from-scratch small plates you won't soon forget, like salted caramel puffs or chicken lollipops. **Known for:** craft cocktails and 170 types of beer; cheese or chocolate fondue; raw bar. $ *Average main: $15* ⊠ *MM 22.5 OS, 22658 Overseas Hwy., Cudjoe Key* ☎ *305/745–8880* ⊕ *www.mynewjoint420lounge.com* ⊙ *Closed Sun. and Mon. No lunch.*

★ Square Grouper Bar and Grill

$$ | SEAFOOD | In an unassuming warehouse-like building on U.S. 1, chef-owner Lynn Bell is creating seafood magic. For starters, try the flash-fried conch with wasabi drizzle or homemade smoked-fish dip. **Known for:** everything made fresh, in-house; long lines in season; outstanding seafood. $ *Average main: $25* ⊠ *MM 22.5 OS, 22658 Overseas Hwy., Cudjoe Key* ☎ *305/745–8880* ⊕ *www.squaregrouperbarandgrill.com* ⊙ *Closed Sun.; Mon. May–Dec.; and Sept.*

☕ Coffee and Quick Bites

Baby's Coffee

$ | AMERICAN | The aroma of rich, roasting coffee beans arrests you at the door of "the Southernmost Coffee Roaster in America." Buy beans by the pound or coffee by the cup, along with sandwiches and sweets. Locals swear it's the best coffee in the Keys and beyond. **Known for:** best coffee in the Keys; gluten-free, vegan, and vegetarian specialty foods; excellent service. $ *Average main: $8* ⊠ *MM 15 OS, 3180 Overseas Hwy., Sugarloaf Key* ☎ *305/744–9866, 800/523–2326* ⊕ *www.babyscoffee.com.*

Hotels

★ Little Palm Island Resort & Spa

$$$$ | RESORT | Haute tropicale best describes this wildly luxurious private-island retreat, and "second mortgage" might explain how some can afford the extravagant prices, but for those who can, it's worth the price. **Pros:** secluded setting; heavenly spa; easy wildlife viewing. **Cons:** expensive; might be too quiet for some; accessible only by boat or seaplane. $ *Rooms from: $1,500* ⊠ *MM 28.5 OS, 28500 Overseas Hwy., Little Torch Key* ☎ *305/872–2524, 800/343–8567* ⊕ *www.littlepalmisland.com* ➭ *30 suites* ◎ *Free Breakfast* ☞ *No one under age 16 allowed on island.*

Looe Key Reef Resort & Dive Center

$ | HOTEL | If your Keys vacation is all about diving, you won't mind the no-frills, basic motel rooms with dated furniture at this scuba-obsessed operation because it's the closest place to the stellar reef to stay. **Pros:** guests get discounts on dive and snorkel trips; inexpensive rates; casual Keys atmosphere. **Cons:** some reports of uncleanliness; unheated pool; close to the road. $ *Rooms from: $159* ⊠ *MM 27.5 OS, 27340 Overseas Hwy., Little Torch Key* ☎ *305/872–2215, 877/816–3483* ⊕ *www.diveflakeys.com* ➭ *24 rooms* ◎ *No Meals.*

Parmer's Resort

$ | HOTEL | Almost every room at this budget-friendly option has a view of South Pine Channel, with the lovely curl of Big Pine Key in the foreground. **Pros:** bright rooms; pretty setting; good value. **Cons:** a bit out of the way; housekeeping costs extra; little shade around the pool. $ *Rooms from: $165* ⊠ *MM 28.7 BS, 565 Barry Ave., Little Torch Key* ☎ *305/872–2157* ⊕ *www.parmersresort.com* ➭ *47 units* ◎ *Free Breakfast.*

Activities

KAYAKING
Sugarloaf Marina

KAYAKING | FAMILY | Rates for one-person kayaks are based on an hourly or daily rental. Two-person kayaks are also available. Delivery is free for rentals of three days or more. The folks at the marina can also hook you up with an outfitter for a day of offshore or backcountry fishing. There's also a well-stocked ship store. ⊠ *MM*

17 BS, 17015 Overseas Hwy., Sugarloaf Key ☏ *305/745–3135* ⊕ *www.sugarloafkeymarina.com* ✉ *From $15 per hr.*

SCUBA DIVING AND SNORKELING

This is the closest you can get on land to Looe Key Reef, which is where local dive operators love to head. In 1744 the HMS *Looe,* a British warship, ran aground and sank on one of the most beautiful coral reefs in the Keys. Today, the key owes its name to the ill-fated ship.

The 5.3-square-nautical-mile reef, part of the Florida Keys National Marine Sanctuary, has strands of elkhorn coral on its eastern margin, as well as purple sea fans and abundant sponges and sea urchins. On its seaward side, it drops almost vertically 50 to 90 feet. In its midst, the Shipwreck Trail plots the location of nine historic wreck sites in 14 to 120 feet of water. Buoys mark the sites, and underwater signs tell the history of each site and what marine life to expect.

Snorkelers and divers will find the sanctuary a quiet place to observe reef life—except in July, when the annual Underwater Music Festival pays homage to Looe Key's beauty and promotes reef awareness with six hours of music broadcast via underwater speakers. Dive shops, charters, and private boats transport about 500 divers and snorkelers to hear the spectacle, which includes classical, jazz, New Age, and Caribbean music, as well as a little Jimmy Buffett. There are even underwater Elvis impersonators.

Looe Key Reef Resort & Dive Center

SCUBA DIVING | **FAMILY** | This center, the closest dive shop to Looe Key Reef, offers two affordable trips daily, at 8 am and 12:45 pm (for divers, snorkelers, or bubble watchers). The maximum depth is 30 feet, so snorkelers and divers go on the same boat. Call to check for availability for wreck and night dives. The dive boat, a 45-foot catamaran, is docked at the full-service Looe Key Reef Resort. ✉ *MM 27.5 OS, 27340 Overseas Hwy., Little Torch Key* ☏ *305/872–2215, 877/816–3483* ⊕ *looekeyreefresort.com* ✉ *From $40.*

KEY WEST

Updated by
Sara Liss

⊙ Sights   🍴 Restaurants   🛏 Hotels   ⬤ Shopping   🍸 Nightlife
★★★★★   ★★★★★   ★★★★★   ★★★★☆   ★★★★☆

WELCOME TO KEY WEST

TOP REASONS TO GO

★ **Watching the sunset:** Revel in both the beautiful sunset and the gutsy performers at Mallory Square's nightly celebration.

★ **The Conch Tour Train:** Hop aboard for a narrated tour of the town's tawdry past and rare architectural treasures.

★ **Barhopping:** Nightlife rules in Key West. Do the "Duval Crawl," the local version of club-hopping. But first fortify yourself at one of the town's exceptional restaurants.

★ **The Hemingway connection:** Visit Ernest Hemingway's historic home for a page out of Key West's literary past.

★ **The Dry Tortugas:** Do a day trip to Dry Tortugas National Park for snorkeling and hiking away from the crowds.

★ **The Historic Seaport:** Stroll this maritime promenade that features restaurants, bars, and art galleries as well as charter fishing boats.

1 Old Town. Most of Key West's attractions, hotels, and restaurants—not to mention bars—are located here. And while it gets very busy and hectic around Duval, there are plenty of quiet streets to stroll down. Don't miss the nightly sunset celebration at Mallory Square.

115

6

Key West WELCOME TO KEY WEST

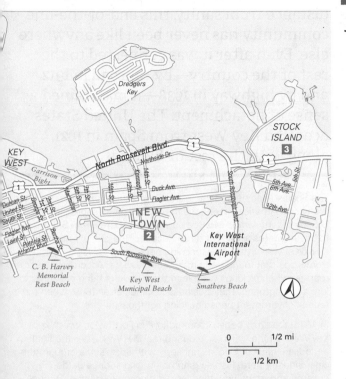

2 **New Town.** While you won't find as much action as you will in Old Town, New Town is a popular place to stay as it offers a wide variety of accommodations, often at lesser rates (most hotels offer shuttles to Old Town). Smathers Beach, Key West's largest strand, is also here.

3 **Stock Island.** This laid-back island harkens back to Old Florida with boatyards, artist studios, the area's last working waterfront, and a mellower vibe than what you'll find in Old Town—though a few upscale hotels, including The Perry and Oceans Edge, have sprung up.

Situated 150 miles from Miami, 90 miles from Havana, and an immeasurable distance from sanity, this end-of-the-line community has never been like anywhere else. Even after it was connected to the rest of the country—by railroad in 1912 and by highway in 1938—it maintained a sense of detachment. The United States acquired Key West from Spain in 1821, along with the rest of Florida.

The Spanish had named the island Cayo Hueso, or Bone Key, after the Native American skeletons they found on its shores. In 1823, U.S. president James Monroe sent Commodore David S. Porter to chase pirates away. For three decades, the primary industry in Key West was wrecking—rescuing people and salvaging cargo from ships that foundered on the nearby reefs. According to some reports, when pickings were lean the wreckers hung out lights to lure ships aground. Their business declined after 1849, when the federal government began building lighthouses.

In 1845, the army began construction on Fort Taylor, which kept Key West on the Union side during the Civil War. After the fighting ended, an influx of Cubans unhappy with Spain's rule brought the cigar industry here. Fishing, shrimping, and sponge gathering became important industries, as did pineapple canning. Throughout much of the 19th century and into the 20th, Key West was Florida's wealthiest city per capita. But in 1929, the local economy began to unravel. Cigar making moved to Tampa, Hawaii dominated the pineapple industry, and the sponges succumbed to blight. Then the Depression hit, and within a few years half the population was on relief.

Tourism began to revive Key West, but that came to a halt when a hurricane knocked out the railroad bridge in 1935. To help the tourism industry recover from that crushing blow, the government offered incentives for islanders to turn their charming homes—many of them built by shipwrights—into guesthouses and inns. That wise foresight has left the town with more than 100 such lodgings, a hallmark of Key West vacationing today. In the 1950s, the discovery of "pink gold" in the Dry Tortugas boosted the economy of the entire region. Catching Key West shrimp required a fleet of up to 500 boats and flooded local restaurants with some of the sweetest shrimp alive. The town's artistic community found inspiration in the colorful fishing boats.

Key West reflects a diverse population: Conchs (natives, many of whom trace their ancestry to the Bahamas); freshwater Conchs (longtime residents who migrated from somewhere else years ago); Latin Americans (primarily Cuban immigrants); recent refugees from the urban sprawl of mainland Florida; military personnel; and an assortment of vagabonds, drifters, and dropouts in search of refuge.

The island was once a gay vacation hot spot, and it remains a decidedly gay-friendly destination. Some of the once-renowned gay guesthouses, however, no longer cater to an exclusively gay clientele. Key Westers pride themselves on their tolerance of all people, all sexual orientations, and even all animals. Most restaurants allow pets, and it's not surprising to see stray cats, dogs, and even chickens roaming freely through the dining rooms. The chicken issue is one that government officials periodically try to bring to an end, but the colorful fowl continue to strut and crow, particularly in the vicinity of Old Town's Bahamian Village.

As a tourist destination, Key West has a lot to offer—an average temperature of 79°F, 19th-century architecture, and a laid-back lifestyle. Yet much has been lost to those eager for a buck. Duval Street is starting to resemble a shopping mall with name-brand storefronts, garish T-shirt shops, and tattoo parlors with sidewalk views of the inked action. Cruise ships dwarf the town's skyline, and day-trippers fill the streets, gawking at the hippies with dogs in their bike baskets and the oddball lot of locals, some of whom bark louder than the dogs.

Planning

When to Go

Key West has a growing calendar of festivals and artistic and cultural events—including the Conch Republic Independence Celebration in April and the Halloween Fantasy Fest in October.

December brings festivity in the form of a lighted boat parade at the Historic Seaport and New Year's Eve revelry that rivals any in the nation. Few cities of its size—a mere 2 miles by 4 miles—celebrate with the joie de vivre of this one.

Getting Here and Around

AIR

You can fly directly to Key West on a limited number of flights, most of which connect at other Florida airports. But a lot of folks fly into Miami or Fort Lauderdale and drive down or take the bus.

BOAT

Key West Express operates air-conditioned ferries between the Key West Terminal (Caroline and Grinnell Streets) and Marco Island and Fort Myers Beach. The trip from Fort Myers Beach takes at least four hours each way and costs $130 one way, $155 round trip. Ferries depart from Fort Myers Beach at 8 am and from Key West at 6 pm. The Marco Island ferry costs $95 one way and $155 round trip and departs at 8 am. A photo ID is required for each passenger. Advance reservations are recommended and can save money.

BUS AND SHUTTLE

Greyhound Lines runs a special Keys Shuttle up to twice a day (depending on the day of the week) from Miami International Airport (departing from Concourse E, lower level) that stops throughout the Keys. Fares run about $45 (online fare) to $57 for Key West. Keys Shuttle runs scheduled service three times a day in 15-passenger vans between Miami Airport and Key West with stops throughout the Keys for $70 to $90 per person. SuperShuttle charges $102 per passenger for trips from Miami International Airport to the Upper Keys. To go farther into the Keys, you must book an entire 11-person van, which costs about $350 to Key West. You need to place your request for transportation back to the airport 24 hours in advance. Uber is also available throughout the Keys and from the airport.

For detailed information on these services, see Air Travel in Travel Smart.

LOCAL BUSES

Between Mile Markers 4 and 0, Key West is the one place in the Keys where you could conceivably do without a car, especially if you plan on staying around Old Town. If you've driven the 106 miles down the chain, you're probably ready to abandon your car in the hotel parking lot anyway. Trolleys, buses, bikes, scooters, and feet are more suitable alternatives. When your feet tire, catch a rickshaw-style pedicab ride, which will run you about $1.50 a minute. But to explore the beaches, New Town, and Stock Island, you'll need a car or taxi.

The City of Key West Department of Transportation has six color-coded bus routes traversing the island from 5:30 am to 11:30 pm. Stops have signs with the international bus symbol. Schedules are available on buses and at hotels, visitor centers, shops, and online. The fare is $2 one way. Its Lower Keys Shuttle bus runs between Marathon to Key West ($4 one way), with scheduled stops along the way.

Hotels

Historic cottages, restored century-old conch houses, and large resorts are among the offerings in Key West. Quaint guesthouses, the town's trademark, offer a true island experience in residential neighborhoods near Old Town's restaurants, shops, and clubs. In high season, Christmas through Easter, it's hard to find a decent room for less than $200, and most places raise prices considerably during holidays and festivals. Many guesthouses and inns do not welcome children under 16, and most do not permit smoking indoors. Most tariffs include an expanded continental breakfast and, often, an afternoon glass of wine or snack.

LODGING ALTERNATIVES

The Lodging Association of the Florida Keys and Key West is an umbrella organization for dozens of local properties. Key West Vacations lists historic cottages, homes, and condominiums for rent. Rent Key West Vacations specializes in renting vacation homes and condos for a week or longer. Vacation Key West lists all kinds of properties. In addition, ⊕ airbnb.com and ⊕ vrbo.com have many offerings.

CONTACTS Lodging Association of the Florida Keys and Key West. ⊠ 818 White St., Ste. 8, Historic Seaport ☎ 800/492–1911 ⊕ www. keyslodging.org. **Key West Vacations.** ☎ 888/775–3993 ⊕ www. keywestvacations.com. **Rent Key West Vacations.** ⊠ 1075 Duval St., Suite C11, Key West ☎ 305/294–0990, 800/833–7368 ⊕ www. rentkeywest.com. **Vacation Key West.** ⊠ Key West Ferry Terminal, 100 Grinnell St., Key West ☎ 305/295–9500, 800/595–5397 ⊕ www.vacationkw.com.

Nightlife

Rest up: much of what happens in Key West occurs after dark. Open your mind and take a stroll. Scruffy street performers strum next to dogs in sunglasses. Characters wearing parrots or iguanas try to sell you your photo with their pet. Brawls tumble out the doors of Sloppy Joe's. Drag queens strut across stages in Joan

Rivers garb. Tattooed men lick whipped cream off women's body parts. And margaritas flow like a Jimmy Buffett tune.

Restaurants

Bring your appetite and a sense of daring. Leave behind any notions about propriety. A meal in Key West can mean overlooking the eccentrics along Duval Street to eat at a colorful, hole-in-the-wall place, watching roosters and pigeons battle for a scrap of food that may have escaped your fork while dining alfresco, relishing the finest in what used to be the dining room of a 19th-century Victorian home, or enjoying a meal while gazing out at boats jockeying for position in the marina.

Seafood dominates local menus, but preparations can range from Cuban and New World to Asian and continental. Citrus and tropical fruits figure prominently, with mango, papaya, and passion fruit often featured in beverages.

Hotel and restaurant reviews have been shortened. For full information visit Fodors.com. Hotel prices are the lowest cost of a standard double room in high season. Restaurant prices are the average cost of a main course at dinner, or if dinner is not served, at lunch.

What It Costs			
$	$$	$$$	$$$$
RESTAURANTS			
under $20	$20–$25	$26–$35	over $35
HOTELS			
under $200	$200–$300	$301–$400	over $400

Shopping

On these streets, you'll find colorful local art of widely varying quality, key limes made into everything imaginable, and the raunchiest T-shirts in the civilized world. Browsing the boutiques—with frequent pub stops along the way—makes for an entertaining stroll down Duval Street. Cocktails certainly help the appreciation of some goods, such as the figurine of a naked man blowing bubbles out his backside or the swashbuckling pirate costumes that are no longer just for Halloween.

Hop aboard the Conch Tour Train for a 90-minute narrated tour of Key West, including Old Town.

Tours

BIKE TOURS
Lloyd's Original Tropical Bike Tour
BICYCLE TOURS | FAMILY | Explore the natural, noncommercial side of Key West at a leisurely pace, stopping on backstreets and in backyards of private homes to sample native fruits and view indigenous plants and trees with a 45-year Key West veteran. The behind-the-scenes tours run two hours and include a bike rental. ⊠ *601 Truman Ave., Key West* ☏ *305/428–2678* ⊕ *www.lloydstrop-icalbiketour.com* ✆ *$49.*

BUS TOURS
★ Conch Tour Train
BUS TOURS | FAMILY | The Conch Tour Train is a 90-minute narrated tour of Key West, traveling 14 miles through Old Town and around the island. Board at Mallory Square or Angela Street and Duval Street depot every half hour from 9 to 4:30. Discount tickets are available online. ⊠ *303 Front St., Historic Seaport* ☏ *305/294–5161, 888/916–8687* ⊕ *www.conchtourtrain.com* ✆ *$40.*

Old Town Trolley
BUS TOURS | FAMILY | Old Town Trolley operates trolley-style buses, departing from Mallory Square every 30 minutes from 9 to 4:30, for 90-minute narrated tours of Key West. The smaller trolleys go places the larger Conch Tour Train won't fit, and you can ride a second consecutive day for an additional $24. You may disembark

at any of 13 stops and reboard a later trolley. You can save nearly $4 by booking online. It also offers package deals with Old Town attractions. ✉ *1 Whitehead St., Old Town* ☎ *305/296–6688, 855/623–8289* ⊕ *www.trolleytours.com/key-west* ✆ *$58*.

NIGHTLIFE TOURS
Best of the Bars
SPECIAL-INTEREST TOURS | Southernmost Scavenger Hunt's "Best of the Bars" challenge has teams of two to five touring the bars of Key West for clues, libations, and prizes. It hosts the event at 7 pm most Fridays, Saturdays, and Sundays, starting at Sloppy Joe's. ✉ *631 Greene St., Historic Seaport* ☎ *305/292–9994* ⊕ *keywest-hunt.com* ✆ *$20*.

RUM TOURS
Papa's Pilar Rum Distillery
SPECIAL-INTEREST TOURS | A beautiful 1879 brick building (formerly a tobacco warehouse) houses the flagship store and tour for Papa Hemingway's rum distillery. Broaden your rum knowledge and let the distiller be your guide, or just quench your thirst for adventure with a tasting. Either way, you'll see lots of Hemingway memorabilia on display and for sale. The Hemingway Foundation gives a portion of the proceeds to causes that Papa was passionate about, like ocean conservation. ✉ *201 Simonton St.* ☎ *305/414–8754* ⊕ *www.papaspilar.com* ✆ *Tour $10*.

WALKING TOURS
Historic Florida Keys Foundation
WALKING TOURS | In addition to publishing several good guides on Key West, the foundation conducts tours of the City Cemetery on Tuesday and Thursday at 9:30 am. ✉ *Old City Hall, 510 Greene St., Key West* ☎ *305/292–6718* ⊕ *www.historicfloridakeys.org* ✆ *$15*.

Key West Promotions
WALKING TOURS | If you're not entirely a do-it-yourselfer, Key West Promotions offers a variety of pub tours, from the famous Duval Crawl to a chilling, haunted, and "spirited" adventure. ✉ *424 Greene St., Key West* ☎ *305/294–7170* ⊕ *www.keywestwalking-tours.com*.

Visitor Information

CONTACTS Greater Key West Chamber of Commerce. ✉ *510 Greene St., 1st fl., Key West* ☎ *305/294–2587, 800/527–8539* ⊕ *www.keywestchamber.org*.

Old Town

The heart of Key West, the historic Old Town area runs from White Street to the waterfront. Beginning in 1822, wharves, warehouses, chandleries, ship-repair facilities, and eventually, in 1891, the U.S. Custom House, sprang up around the deep harbor to accommodate the navy's large ships and other sailing vessels. Wreckers, merchants, and sea captains built lavish houses near the bustling waterfront.

A remarkable number of these fine Victorian and pre-Victorian structures have been restored to their original grandeur and now serve as homes, guesthouses, shops, restaurants, and museums. These, along with the dwellings of famous writers, artists, and politicians who've come to Key West over the past 175 years, are among the area's approximately 3,000 historic structures.

Old Town also has the city's finest restaurants and hotels, lively street life, and popular nightspots. The Historic Seaport is worth a stroll to check out its restaurants, bars, and galleries and to sign up for a boat tour.

TIMING

Allow two full days to see all the Old Town museums and homes, especially if you plan to peruse the shops. For a narrated trip on the tour train or trolley, budget an hour to ride the loop without getting off and an entire day if you plan to get off and on at some of the sights and restaurants.

Sights

Audubon House & Tropical Gardens

GARDEN | If you've ever seen an engraving by ornithologist John James Audubon, you'll understand why his name is synonymous with birds. See his works in this three-story house, which was built in the 1840s for Captain John Geiger and is filled with period furniture. It now commemorates Audubon's 1832 stop in Key West while he was traveling through Florida to study birds. After an introduction by a docent, you can do a self-guided tour of the house and gardens. An art gallery sells lithographs of the artist's famed portraits. ⊠ *205 Whitehead St., Old Town* ☎ *305/294–2116, 877/294–2470* ⊕ *www.audubonhouse.com* 💲 *$15.*

Dry Tortugas National Park Historic Interpretive Center and the Historic Key West Bight

HISTORY MUSEUM | **FAMILY** | If you can't make it out to see Fort Jefferson in Dry Tortugas National Park, this is the next best thing.

A Good Tour

You can do this tour via the Old Town Trolley or the Conch Tour Train, but Old Town is also manageable on foot, bicycle, moped, or electric car. However, the area is expansive, so pick and choose from the stops on this tour, or break it into two or more days.

Start on Whitehead Street at the **Ernest Hemingway Home and Museum**, then cross the street and climb to the top of the **Key West Lighthouse Museum and Keeper's Quarters** for a spectacular view.

Return to Whitehead Street and follow it north to Angela Street, where you'll turn right. At Margaret Street, the **Key West Cemetery** is worth a look for its aboveground vaults and unusual headstone inscriptions. Head north on Margaret Street, turn left onto Southard Street, and follow it through Truman Annex to **Fort Zachary Taylor Historic State Park**. Right before you get to Truman Annex, stop in for a drink at the **Green Parrot Bar**, which has been serving locals since 1890, at the corner of Southard Street and Whitehead.

Walk west into Truman Annex to see the **Harry S. Truman Little White House**, President Truman's vacation residence. Return east on Caroline and turn left on Whitehead to visit the **Audubon House and Tropical Gardens,** honoring the famed artist and naturalist. Follow Whitehead north to Greene Street and turn left to see the salvaged sea treasures of the **Mel Fisher Maritime Museum**. At Whitehead's northern end are the **Key West Aquarium** and the **Key West Museum of Art and History,** in the former historic U.S. Custom House.

By late afternoon you should be ready to cool off with a dip or catch a few rays at the beach. From the aquarium, head east on Whitehead Street about 1½ miles to the Southernmost Point for a famed photo op before continuing on South Street. Turn right on Vernon, following it to Waddell Street and **Dog Beach**, which, as it's name suggests, is dog-friendly. A little farther east is **Higgs Beach–Astro City**, on Atlantic Boulevard between White and Reynolds Streets.

As the sun starts to sink, return to the north end of Old Town and follow the crowds to Mallory Square to watch Key West's nightly sunset spectacle. For dinner, head east on Caroline Street to the **Historic Seaport** at the Key West Bight.

The former Custom House is now a museum focusing on Key West's fascinating history.

Opened in 2013 by the national park's official ferry commissioner, this free attraction in Key West's Historic Seaport has an impressive (1:87) scale model of the fort; life-size figures, including one of the fort's most famous prisoners, Dr. Samuel Mudd (who was involved in the conspiracy to assassinate Abraham Lincoln); and a Junior Ranger station for the little ones, with hands-on educational fun. The exhibits are housed in a historic site as well: the old Thompson Fish House, where local fishermen once brought their daily catch for processing. ✉ *901 Caroline St., Historic Seaport* ☎ *305/294–7009* ⊕ *www.drytortugas.com* ✉ *Free.*

★ The Ernest Hemingway Home & Museum

HISTORIC HOME | Amusing anecdotes spice up the guided tours of Ernest Hemingway's home, built in 1851 by the town's most successful wrecker. While living here between 1931 and 1942, Hemingway wrote about 70% of his life's work, including classics like *For Whom the Bell Tolls*. Few of his belongings remain aside from some books, and there's little about his actual work, but photographs help you visualize his day-to-day life. The famous six-toed descendants of Hemingway's cats—many named for actors, artists, authors, and even a hurricane—have free rein of the property. Tours begin every 10 minutes and take 30 minutes; then you're free to explore on your own. Be sure to find out why there is a urinal in the garden! ✉ *907 Whitehead St., Old Town* ☎ *305/294–1136* ⊕ *www.hemingwayhome.com* ✉ *$17.*

Old Town–North of Angela Street

Felming Key Cut

Key West Bight

Sunset Key

| 0 | 1,000 ft |
| 0 | 200 m |

KEY

1 Exploring Sights

1 Restaurants

1 Hotels

Sights

Audubon House & Tropical Gardens, **6**

Dry Tortugas National Park Historic Interpretive Center and the Historic Key West Bight, **11**

Florida Keys Eco-Discovery Center, **8**

Harry S. Truman Little White House, **7**

Historic Seaport at the Key West Bight, **12**

Key West Aquarium, **2**

Key West Library, **10**

Key West Museum of Art & History, **4**

Key West Shipwreck Treasure Museum, **3**

Mallory Square and Pier, **1**

Mel Fisher Maritime Museum, **5**

Nancy Forrester's Secret Garden, **9**

Restaurants

Azur Restaurant, **12**

Bistro 245, **2**

B.O.'s Fish Wagon, **10**

The Cafe, **6**

Café Marquesa, **9**

Café Solé, **13**

Conch Republic Seafood Company, **4**

El Meson de Pepe, **3**

Half Shell Raw Bar, **11**

Jimmy Buffett's Margaritaville, **5**

Latitudes, **1**

Mangia Mangia, **14**

Onlywood Pizzeria, **7**

Sarabeth's Key West, **8**

Hotels

Ambrosia Key West, **9**

Crowne Plaza La Concha, **7**

Eden House, **15**

The Grand Maloney, **5**

Island City House Hotel, **12**

Island House, **16**

Key West Bed and Breakfast/The Popular House, **11**

The Marker, **13**

Marquesa Hotel, **8**

NYAH: Not Your Average Hotel, **10**

Ocean Key Resort & Spa, **3**

Opal Key Resort & Marina, **4**

Pier House Resort & Spa, **2**

Simonton Court, **6**

Sunset Key Cottages, **1**

Westwinds Inn, **14**

★ Florida Keys Eco-Discovery Center

OTHER MUSEUM | FAMILY | While visiting Fort Zachary Taylor Historic State Park, stop in at this colorful, 6,400-square-foot, interactive attraction, where you can experience a variety of Florida Keys habitats from pinelands, beach dunes, and mangroves to the deep sea. Walk through a model of the *Aquarius*—a unique, underwater, National Oceanic and Atmospheric Administration (NOAA) laboratory 9 miles off Key Largo—to virtually discover what lurks in the ocean's depths. Touch-screen computer displays, a dramatic movie, a 2,500-gallon aquarium, and live underwater web cameras show off North America's only contiguous barrier coral reef. You'll leave with a new understanding of the native animals and unique plants of the Florida Keys. ⊠ *35 E. Quay Rd., Old Town* ⌖ *At end of Southard St. in Truman Annex* ☎ *305/809–4750* ⊕ *eco-discovery.com* ⊠ *Free (donations accepted)* ⊗ *Closed Sun. and Mon.*

★ Fort Zachary Taylor Historic State Park

MILITARY SIGHT | FAMILY | Construction of the redbrick fort began in 1845 but was halted during the Civil War. Even though Florida seceded from the Union, Yankee forces used the fort as a base to block Confederate shipping. More than 1,500 Confederate vessels were detained in Key West's harbor. The fort, completed in 1866, was also used in the Spanish-American War. Take a 30-minute guided walking tour of this National Historic Landmark at noon and 2 or do a self-guided tour anytime between 8 and 5. One of the park's most popular features is its man-made beach, a rest stop for migrating birds in the spring and fall; there are also picnic areas, hiking and biking trails, and a kayak launch. ⊠ *Old Town* ⌖ *End of Southard St., through Truman Annex* ☎ *305/292–6713* ⊕ *www.floridastateparks.org/park/Fort-Taylor* ⊠ *From $5.*

Harry S. Truman Little White House

HISTORIC HOME | Renovations to this circa-1890 landmark have restored the home and gardens to the Truman era, down to the wallpaper pattern. A free photographic review of visiting dignitaries and presidents—John F. Kennedy, Jimmy Carter, and Bill Clinton are among the chief executives who passed through here—is on display in the back of the gift shop. Engaging 45-minute tours, conducted every 20 minutes, start with an excellent 10-minute video on the history of the property and Truman's visits. On the grounds of Truman Annex, a 103-acre former military parade grounds and barracks, the home served as a "winter White House" for presidents Truman, Eisenhower, and Kennedy. Entry is cheaper when purchased in advance online; tickets bought on-site add sales tax. ■TIP→ **The house tour does require climbing steps. Note that you can also do a free self-guided botanical tour of the grounds with a brochure from the museum store.** ⊠ *111 Front St.,*

Classics like *For Whom the Bell Tolls* were written at the Ernest Hemingway Home and Museum.

Old Town ☎ *305/294–9911* ⊕ *www.trumanlittlewhitehouse.com* ✉ *$24* ☞ *Last tour at 4:30 pm.*

Historic Seaport at the Key West Bight

MARINA/PIER | What was once a funky—in some places even seedy—part of town is now a 20-acre historic district with restored structures containing waterfront restaurants, open-air bars, museums, clothing stores, and water-sports concessions. It's all linked by the 2-mile waterfront Harborwalk, which runs between Front and Grinnell Streets, passing big ships, schooners, sunset cruises, fishing charters, and glass-bottom boats. This is where the locals go for great music and good drinks. ✉ *Historic Seaport* ⊕ *www.keywesthistoricseaport.com.*

Key West Aquarium

AQUARIUM | **FAMILY** | Pet a nurse shark and explore the fascinating underwater realm of the Keys without getting wet at this historic aquarium. Hundreds of tropical fish and enormous sea creatures live here—all locals. A touch tank enables you to handle starfish, sea cucumbers, horseshoe and hermit crabs, and even horse and queen conchs—living totems of the Conch Republic. Built in 1934 by the Works Progress Administration as the world's first open-air aquarium, most of the building has been enclosed for all-weather viewing. Guided tours, included in the admission price, feature shark feedings. Tickets are cheaper when booked online. ✉ *1 Whitehead St., Old Town* ☎ *305/296-2051* ⊕ *www.keywestaquarium.com* ✉ *$22.*

Hemingway Was Here

In a town where Pulitzer Prize–winning writers are almost as common as coconuts, Ernest Hemingway stands out. Many bars and restaurants around the island claim that he ate or drank there.

Hemingway came to Key West in 1928 at the urging of writer John Dos Passos and rented a house with his second wife, Pauline Pfeiffer. They spent winters in the Keys and summers in Europe and Wyoming, occasionally taking African safaris. Along the way, they had two sons, Patrick and Gregory. In 1931, Pauline's wealthy uncle Gus gave the couple the house at 907 Whitehead Street. Now known as the Ernest Hemingway Home and Museum, it's Key West's number one tourist attraction. Renovations included the addition of a pool and a tropical garden.

In 1935, when the visitor bureau included the house in a tourist brochure, Hemingway promptly built the brick wall that surrounds it today. He wrote of the visitor bureau's offense in a 1935 essay for *Esquire,* saying, "The house at present occupied by your correspondent is listed as number eighteen in a compilation of the forty-eight things for a tourist to see in Key West. So there will be no difficulty in a tourist finding it or any other of the sights of the city, a map has been prepared by the local F.E.R.A. authorities to be presented to each arriving visitor. This is all very flattering to the easily bloated ego of your correspondent but very hard on production."

During his time in Key West, Hemingway penned some of his most important works, including *A Farewell to Arms, To Have and Have Not, Green Hills of Africa,* and *Death in the Afternoon.* His rigorous schedule consisted of writing almost every morning in his second-story studio above the pool, then promptly descending the stairs at midday. By afternoon and evening he was ready for drinking, fishing, swimming, boxing, and hanging around with the boys.

One close friend was Joe Russell, a craggy fisherman and owner of the rugged bar Sloppy Joe's, originally at 428 Greene Street but now at 201 Duval Street. Russell was the only one in town who would cash Hemingway's $1,000 royalty check. Russell and Charles Thompson introduced Hemingway to deep-sea fishing, which became fodder for his writing.

Hemingway stayed in Key West for 11 years before leaving Pauline for his third wife. Pauline and the boys stayed on in the house, which sold in 1951 for $80,000, 10 times its original cost.

The Key West Butterfly & Nature Conservatory

GARDEN | FAMILY | This air-conditioned refuge for butterflies, birds, and humans gladdens the soul with hundreds of colorful wings—more than 45 species of butterflies alone—in a lovely glass-encased bubble. Waterfalls, artistic benches, paved pathways, birds, and lush, flowering vegetation elevate this above most butterfly attractions. The gift shop and gallery are worth a visit on their own. ⊠ 1316 Duval St., Old Town ☎ 305/296–2988, 800/839–4647 ⊕ www.keywestbutterfly.com ☞ $15.

Key West Cemetery

CEMETERY | You can learn almost as much about a town's history through its cemetery as through its historic houses. Key West's celebrated 20-acre burial place may leave you wanting more, with headstone epitaphs such as "I told you I was sick" and, for a wayward husband, "Now I know where he's sleeping at night." Among the interesting plots are a memorial to the sailors killed in the sinking of the battleship USS Maine, carved angels and lambs marking graves of children, and grand aboveground crypts that put to shame many of the town's dwellings for the living. There are separate plots for Catholics, Jews, and refugees from Cuba. You're free to walk around the cemetery on your own, but the best way to see it is on a 90-minute tour given by the staff and volunteers of the Historic Florida Keys Foundation. Tours leave from the main gate, and reservations are required. ⊠ Margaret and Angela Sts., Old Town ☎ 305/292–6718 ⊕ www.historicfloridakeys.org ☞ Tours $15.

Key West Garden Club at West Martello Tower

GARDEN | For over 65 years, the Key West Garden Club has maintained lush gardens among the arches and ruins of this redbrick Civil War–era fort. You can see the impressive collection of native and tropical plants while meandering past fountains, sculptures, and a picture-perfect gazebo on a self-guided tour. The garden hosts art, orchid, and flower shows February through April, and volunteers lead private garden tours one weekend in March. ⊠ 1100 Atlantic Blvd., Old Town ✛ Where White St. and the Atlantic Ocean meet ☎ 305/294–3210 ⊕ www.keywestgardenclub.com ☞ Free (donations welcome).

Key West Library

LIBRARY | Check out the pretty palm garden next to the Key West Library, just off Duval Street. This leafy, outdoor reading area, with shaded benches, is the perfect place to escape the frenzy and crowds of Old Town. There's free Internet access in the library, too. ⊠ 700 Fleming St., Old Town ☎ 305/292–3595 ⊕ www.keyslibraries.org ⊗ Closed Sun.

Key West Lighthouse & Keeper's Quarters

LIGHTHOUSE | FAMILY | For the best view in town, climb the 88 steps to the top of this 1847 lighthouse. The 92-foot structure has a Fresnel lens, which was installed in the 1860s at a cost of $1 million. The keeper lived in the adjacent 1887 clapboard house, which now exhibits vintage photographs, ship models, nautical charts, and artifacts from all along Key West's reefs. A kids' room is stocked with books and toys. ⊠ *938 Whitehead St., Old Town* ☎ *305/294–0012* ⊕ *www.kwahs.com* ⊠ *$17.*

★ Key West Museum of Art & History

ART MUSEUM | When Key West was designated a U.S. port of entry in the early 1820s, a customhouse was established. Salvaged cargoes from ships wrecked on the reefs were brought here, setting the stage for Key West to become—for a time—the richest city in Florida. The imposing redbrick-and-terra-cotta Richardsonian Romanesque–style building became a museum and art gallery in 1999. Smaller galleries have long-term and changing exhibits about the history of Key West, including a Hemingway room and a permanent Henry Flagler exhibit that commemorates the arrival of Flagler's railroad in Key West in 1912. ⊠ *281 Front St., Old Town* ☎ *305/295–6616* ⊕ *www.kwahs.com* ⊠ *$13.*

Key West Shipwreck Treasure Museum

HISTORY MUSEUM | FAMILY | Much of Key West's history, early prosperity, and interesting architecture come from ships that ran aground on its coral reef. Artifacts from the circa-1856 *Isaac Allerton,* which yielded $150,000 worth of wreckage, comprise the museum portion of this multifaceted attraction. Actors and films add a bit of Disneyesque drama. The final highlight is climbing to the top of the 65-foot lookout tower, a reproduction of the 20 or so towers used by Key West wreckers during the town's salvaging heyday. ⊠ *1 Whitehead St., Old Town* ☎ *305/292–8990* ⊕ *www. keywestshipwreck.com* ⊠ *$18.*

Mallory Square and Pier

MARINA/PIER | For cruise-ship passengers, this is the disembarkation point for an attack on Key West. For practically every visitor, it's the requisite venue for a nightly sunset celebration that includes street performers—human statues, sword swallowers, tightrope walkers, musicians, and more—plus craft vendors, conch-fritter fryers, and other regulars who defy classification. With all the activity, don't forget to watch the main show: a dazzling tropical sunset. ⊠ *Old Town.*

★ Mel Fisher Maritime Museum

OTHER MUSEUM | FAMILY | In 1622, a flotilla of Spanish galleons laden with riches left Havana en route to Spain, but it foundered in a hurricane 40 miles west of the Keys. In 1985, diver Mel Fisher recovered items from two of the lost ships, including the *Nuestra Señora de Atocha*, said to carry the mother lode of the treasure, and the *Santa Margarita*. Fisher's adventures tracking these fabled hoards and battling the state of Florida for rights are as amazing as the loot you'll see, touch, and learn about in this museum. Artifacts include a 77.76-carat natural emerald worth almost $250,000. Changing second-floor exhibits cover other aspects of Florida maritime history. ⊠ *200 Greene St., Old Town* ☎ *305/294–2633* ⊕ *www.melfisher.org* ⛁ *$17.50.*

Nancy Forrester's Secret Garden

GARDEN | FAMILY | A few blocks from the parties of Duval Street lies a purely selfless labor of love: a backyard garden whose paths lead to colorful (and happily squawking) rescued parrots and macaws. Step inside the nondescript side gate, and you'll meet Nancy, an environmental artist, and her flock of feathered children (which you can hold and feed). At 10 am she personally gives a tour, or come between 11 and 3 and do the self-guided version. Bring a lunch and have a picnic in the shade, or just meander and learn. It's Parroting 101, and it might just be the most memorable day of your Key West vacation. ⊠ *518 Elizabeth St., Old Town* ⊹ *Between Southard and Fleming St.* ☎ *305/294–0015* ⊕ *nancy-forrester.com* ⛁ *$10* ☞ *Leashed dogs are welcome.*

The Southernmost Point

OTHER ATTRACTION | FAMILY | Possibly the most photographed site in Key West (even though the actual geographic southernmost point in the continental United States lies across the bay on a naval base, where you see a satellite dish), this is a must-see. Have your picture taken next to the big striped buoy that's been marking the southernmost point in the continental United States since 1983. A plaque next to it honors Cubans who lost their lives trying to escape to America, and other signs tell Key West history. ⊠ *Whitehead and South Sts., Old Town.*

 Beaches

Dog Beach

BEACH | FAMILY | Next to Louie's Backyard restaurant, this tiny beach—the only one in Key West where dogs are allowed unleashed—has a shore that's a mix of sand and rocks. **Amenities:** none. **Best for:** walking. ⊠ *Vernon and Waddell Sts., Old Town* ⛁ *Free.*

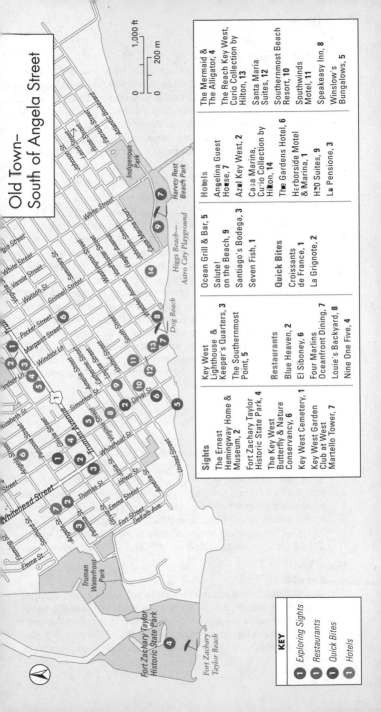

Old Town–
South of Angela Street

0   1,000 ft
0   200 m

Sights

The Ernest
Hemingway Home &
Museum, 2

Fort Zachary Taylor
Historic State Park, 4

The Key West
Butterfly & Nature
Conservancy, 6

Key West Cemetery, 1

Key West Garden
Club at West
Martello Tower, 7

Key West
Lighthouse &
Keeper's Quarters, 3

The Southernmost
Point, 5

Restaurants

Blue Heaven, 2

El Siboney, 6

Four Marlins
Oceanfront Dining, 7

Louie's Backyard, 8

Nine One Five, 4

Ocean Grill & Bar, 5

Salute!
on the Beach, 9

Santiago's Bodega, 3

Seven Fish, 1

Quick Bites

Croissants
de France, 1

La Grignote, 2

Hotels

Angelina Guest
House, 7

Azul Key West, 2

Casa Marina,
Curio Collection by
Hilton, 14

The Gardens Hotel, 6

Herborside Motel
& Marina, 1

H2O Suites, 9

La Pensione, 3

The Mermaid &
The Alligator, 4

The Reach Key West,
Curio Collection by
Hilton, 13

Santa Maria
Suites, 12

Southernmost Beach
Resort, 10

Southwinds
Motel, 11

Speakeasy Inn, 8

Winslow's
Bungalows, 5

KEY

● Exploring Sights
● Restaurants
● Quick Bites
● Hotels

★ Fort Zachary Taylor Beach

BEACH | **FAMILY** | This beach in the historic state park with the same name is the best and safest place to swim in Key West. There's an adjoining picnic area with barbecue grills and shade trees, a snack bar, and rental equipment, including snorkeling gear. A café serves sandwiches and other munchies. Water shoes are recommended since the bottom is rocky here. **Amenities:** food and drink; showers; toilets; water sports. **Best for:** snorkeling; swimming. ⊠ *Old Town ✛ End of Southard St., through Truman Annex* ☎ *305/292–6713* ⊕ *www.fortzacharytaylor.com* ⌷ *From $5.*

★ Higgs Beach and Astro City Playground

BEACH | **FAMILY** | This Monroe County park, with its groomed pebbly sand, is a popular sunbathing spot. A nearby grove of Australian pines provides shade, and the West Martello Tower provides shelter should a storm suddenly sweep in. Kayak and beach-chair rentals are available, as is a volleyball net. The beach also has the largest AIDS memorial in the country and a cultural exhibit commemorating the grave site of 295 enslaved Africans who died after being rescued from three South America–bound slave ships in 1860. An athletic trail with 10 fitness stations is also available. Hungry? Grab a bite to eat at Salute!, the on-site restaurant. Across the street, Astro City Playground is popular with young children. **Amenities:** parking; toilets; water sports. **Best for:** snorkeling; swimming. ⊠ *Atlantic Blvd. between White and Reynolds Sts., Old Town* ⌷ *Free.*

🍴 Restaurants

Azur Restaurant

$$$ | **ECLECTIC** | In a contemporary setting with indoor and outdoor seating, welcoming staff serve original, eclectic dishes that stand out from those at the hordes of Key West restaurants. Key lime–stuffed French toast and yellowtail snapper Benedict make breakfast a pleasant wake-up call; the crab cake BLT commands notice on the lunch menu. **Known for:** homemade gnocchi; a nice variety of fish specials at dinner; daily brunch. ⑤ *Average main: $26* ⊠ *425 Grinnell St., Old Town* ☎ *305/292–2987* ⊕ *www.azur-keywest.com.*

Bistro 245

$$$ | **SEAFOOD** | The sunset views alone are worth a visit, but the food here is stellar as well. Enjoy a key lime martini at the bar or a seafood dinner in the air-conditioned dining room or on the open-air patio. **Known for:** upstairs bar overlooking Mallory Square; Key West pink shrimp; popular weekend brunch. ⑤ *Average main: $35*

✉ *Opal Key Resort & Marina, 245 Front St., Old Town* ☎ *305/294–4000* ⊕ *www.bistro245.com.*

Blue Heaven

$$ | **CARIBBEAN** | The outdoor dining area here is often referred to as "the quintessential Keys experience," and it's hard to argue. There's much to like about this historic Caribbean-style restaurant where Hemingway refereed boxing matches and customers cheered for cockfights. **Known for:** shrimp and grits; lobster Benedict with key lime hollandaise; the wait for a table and lack of parking. ⑤ *Average main: $24* ✉ *729 Thomas St., Old Town* ☎ *305/296–8666* ⊕ *www.blueheavenkw.com* ⊘ *Closed for 6 wks after Labor Day.*

★ B.O.'s Fish Wagon

$ | **SEAFOOD** | What started out as a fish house on wheels appears to have broken down on the corner of Caroline and William Streets and is today one of Key West's junkyard-chic dining institutions. Step up to the window and order a grouper sandwich fried or grilled and topped with key lime sauce. **Known for:** lots of Key West charm; Friday-night jam sessions; all seating on picnic tables in the yard. ⑤ *Average main: $18* ✉ *801 Caroline St., Old Town* ☎ *305/294–9272* ⊕ *bosfishwagon.com.*

The Cafe

$ | **VEGETARIAN** | You don't have to be a vegetarian to love this new-age café decorated with bright artwork and a corrugated-tin-fronted counter. Local favorites include homemade soup, veggie sandwiches and burgers (order them with a side of sweet-potato fries), grilled portobello mushroom salad, seafood, stir-fry dinners, and grilled veggie pizzas. **Known for:** vegan options; homemade sangria; weekend brunch. ⑤ *Average main: $11* ✉ *509 Southard St., Old Town* ☎ *305/296–5515* ⊕ *www.thecafekw.com.*

★ Café Marquesa

$$$ | **EUROPEAN** | You'll find seven or more inspired entrées on a changing menu each night, including anything from yellowtail snapper to seared duck breast. End your meal on a sweet note with chocolate pot de crème and homemade ice cream. **Known for:** relaxed but elegant setting; good wine and martini lists; desserts worth ordering. ⑤ *Average main: $30* ✉ *600 Fleming St., Old Town* ☎ *305/292–1244* ⊕ *marquesa.com/cafe-marquesa* ⊘ *No lunch.*

Café Solé

$$$ | **FRENCH** | This little corner of France hides behind a high wall in a residential neighborhood. Inside, French training intertwines with local ingredients, creating delicious takes on classics, including a must-try conch carpaccio and some of the best bouillabaisse that you'll find outside Marseilles. **Known for:** hogfish in several different preparations; intimate, romantic atmosphere; award-winning key lime pie. ⑤ *Average main: $28* ⊠ *1029 Southard St., Old Town* ☎ *305/294–0230* ⊕ *www.cafesole.com.*

Conch Republic Seafood Company

$$ | SEAFOOD | FAMILY | Because of its location where the fast ferry docks, Conch Republic does a brisk business. It's huge, open-air, and on the water, and the menu is ambitious, offering more than just standard seafood fare. **Known for:** "Royal Reds" peel-and-eat shrimp; no reservations; live music most nights. ⑤ *Average main: $25* ⊠ *631 Greene St., at Elizabeth St., Historic Seaport* ☎ *305/294–4403* ⊕ *www.conchrepublicseafood.com.*

El Meson de Pepe

$ | CUBAN | This is the place to dine—alfresco or in the dining room—on refined Cuban classics. Begin with a megasize mojito while you browse the expansive menu offering *tostones rellenos* (green plantains with different traditional fillings), ceviche, and more. **Known for:** authentic plantain chips; Latin band during the nightly sunset celebration; touristy atmosphere. ⑤ *Average main: $19* ⊠ *Mallory Sq., 410 Wall St., Old Town* ☎ *305/295–2620* ⊕ *www.elmesondepepe.com.*

El Siboney

$ | CUBAN | At this family-style restaurant, the dining room bustles, the food is traditional *cubano,* the prices are reasonable, and the sangria is *muy buena.* There are well-seasoned black beans, a memorable paella, traditional *ropa vieja,* and local seafood served grilled, stuffed, or breaded. **Known for:** memorable paella and traditional dishes; wine and beer only; cheaper than more touristy options close to Duval. ⑤ *Average main: $11* ⊠ *900 Catherine St., Old Town* ☎ *305/296–4184* ⊕ *www.elsiboneyrestaurant.com.*

Four Marlins Oceanfront Dining

$$$ | SEAFOOD | Inspired by an Ernest Hemingway photograph of a family fishing trip in Key West, this oceanfront spot pays homage to pristine seafood that's served alongside views that will make you feel like you're on a luxury liner. While the indoor dining room has a bright and airy feel with nautical decor, the outdoor patio is the spot to reserve, a fitting backdrop to dishes of wood-roasted oysters with smoky lemon, Key West pink shrimp, or grits and vegetable island curry. **Known for:** well-trained staff; craft cocktails; fabulous key lime pie. ⑤ *Average main: $31* ⊠ *The Reach Key West Hotel, 1435 Simonton St., Old Town* ☎ *305/293–6250.*

Half Shell Raw Bar

$ | SEAFOOD | FAMILY | Smack-dab on the docks, this legendary place gets its name from the oysters, clams, and peel-and-eat shrimp that are the stars of its seafood-based menu. It's not clever recipes or fine dining (or even air-conditioning) that packs 'em in; it's fried fish, po'boy sandwiches, and seafood combos. **Known for:** daily happy hour with food and drink deals; few nonseafood options; good people-watching spot. $ *Average main: $16* ⊠ *Lands End Village at Historic Seaport, 231 Margaret St., Historic Seaport* ☎ *305/294–7496* ⊕ *www.halfshellrawbar.com.*

Jimmy Buffett's Margaritaville

$ | AMERICAN | If you must have your cheeseburger in paradise, it may as well be here. The first of Buffett's line of chain eateries, it belongs in Key West more than anywhere else, but, quite frankly, it's more about the name, music, and attitude (and margaritas) than the food. **Known for:** pricey Caribbean bar food; good and spicy conch chowder; raucous party atmosphere most of the time. $ *Average main: $18* ⊠ *500 Duval St., Old Town* ☎ *305/292–1435* ⊕ *www.margaritavillekeywest.com.*

★ Latitudes

$$$ | ECLECTIC | Take the short boat ride to lovely Sunset Key for lunch or dinner on the beach, where the magical views are matched by a stellar menu. At dinner, start with the crispy lobster-crab cakes, then move on to one of the creative entrées, such as seared scallops with spiced butternut squash. **Known for:** amazing sunset views; sophisticated atmosphere and expensive food; lobster bisque. $ *Average main: $32* ⊠ *Sunset Key Guest Cottages, 245 Front St., Old Town* ☎ *305/292–5300, 888/477–7786* ⊕ *www.sunsetkeycottages.com/latitudes-key-west* ⌖ *Reservations are required for the ferry: no reservation, no ride.*

Louie's Backyard

$$$$ | ECLECTIC | Feast your eyes on a steal-your-breath-away view and beautifully presented dishes prepared by executive chef Doug Shook. Once you get over sticker shock on the seasonally changing menu, settle in on the outside deck and enjoy dishes like cracked conch with mango chutney, lamb chops with sun-dried-tomato relish, and tamarind-glazed duck breast. **Known for:** fresh, pricey seafood and steaks; affordable lunch menu; late night drinks at the Afterdeck Bar, directly on the water. $ *Average main: $38* ⊠ *700 Waddell Ave., Old Town* ☎ *305/294–1061* ⊕ *www.louiesbackyard.com.*

Mangia Mangia

$$ | ITALIAN | This longtime favorite serves large portions of homemade pastas that can be matched with any of the homemade sauces. Tables are arranged in a brick garden hung with twinkling lights and in a cozy, casual dining room in an old house. **Known for:** extensive wine list with a nice range of prices; gluten-free and organic pastas; outdoor seating in the garden. $ *Average main: $24* ⊠ *900 Southard St., Old Town* ☎ *305/294–2469* ⊕ *www. mangia-mangia.com* ☾ *No lunch.*

★ Nine One Five

$$$ | ECLECTIC | Twinkling lights draped along the lower- and upper-level porches of a 100-year-old Victorian home set an unstuffy and comfortable stage here. If you like to sample and sip, you'll appreciate the variety of small-plate selections and wines by the glass. **Known for:** fun place to people-watch; intimate and inviting atmosphere; light jazz during dinner. $ *Average main: $32* ⊠ *915 Duval St., Old Town* ☎ *305/296–0669* ⊕ *www.915duval.com* ☾ *No lunch Mon. and Tues.*

Ocean Grill & Bar

$$$ | SEAFOOD | Whether it's breakfast, lunch, or dinner, Ocean Grill serves up fresh Key West seafood in good portions at fair prices. The "Scalouper" is just of one the unique offerings: jumbo diver scallops sliced on the diagonal and served atop pan-seared, local black grouper with a mint puree—sounds odd, but it tastes delightfully fresh. **Known for:** shrimp and grits; bottomless Bloody Marys and mimosas every day 9–3:30; creamy lobster bisque. $ *Average main: $30* ⊠ *1075 Duval St., Old Town* ✛ *Between Duval and Simonton in the Duval Square Mall* ☎ *305/296–4300* ⊕ *www.oceangrillandbar.com.*

Onlywood Pizzeria

$$ | ITALIAN | FAMILY | Pizzas are the star of the show at this bustling trattoria a short walk from the Duval fray. The kitchen churns out a variety of Neopolitan pies from its 2-ton wood-fired oven made of bricks and stones from Mt. Vesuvius. **Known for:** brick-oven pizza; another location near the harbor; burrata salad. $ *Average main: $22* ⊠ *613½ Duval St, Historic Seaport* ☎ *305/735–4412* ⊕ *www. onlywoodkw.com.*

Salute! on the Beach

$$ | ITALIAN | Sister restaurant to Blue Heaven, this colorful establishment sits on Higgs Beach, giving it one of the island's best lunch views—and a bit of sand and salt spray on a windy day. The intriguing menu is Italian with a Caribbean flair and will not disappoint. **Known for:** amazing water views; casual, inviting atmosphere; pricey slice of key lime pie. $ *Average main: $22* ⊠ *Higgs Beach, 1000 Atlantic Blvd., Old Town* ☎ *305/292–1117* ⊕ *www.saluteonthebeach.com.*

★ Santiago's Bodega

$ | SPANISH | Picky palates will be satisfied at this funky, dark, and sensuous tapas restaurant, which is well off the main drag and is a secret spot for local foodies in the know. Small plates include yellowfin tuna ceviche with hunks of avocado and mango or filet mignon with creamy Gorgonzola butter. **Known for:** legendary bread pudding; homemade white or red sangria; a favorite with local chefs. $ *Average main: $16* ⌂ *Bahama Village, 207 Petronia St., Old Town* ☎ *305/296–7691* ⊕ *www.santiagosbodega.com.*

Sarabeth's Key West

$$ | AMERICAN | Named for the award-winning jam-maker and pastry chef Sarabeth Levine, this locally owned restaurant serves all-day breakfast, best enjoyed in the picket-fenced front yard of a circa-1870 synagogue. Lemon ricotta pancakes, pumpkin waffles, and homemade jams make the meal. **Known for:** brunch and dessert; daily specials; key lime pie French toast. $ *Average main: $20* ⌂ *530 Simonton St., at Souhard St., Old Town* ☎ *305/293–8181* ⊕ *www.sarabethskw.com* ⊙ *Closed Mon. and Tues.*

Seven Fish

$$$$ | SEAFOOD | This local hot spot has a casual Key West vibe and an eclectic menu. The specialty is the local fish of the day (like snapper with creamy Thai curry), but you might also try the tropical shrimp salsa, wild-mushroom quesadilla, or old-fashioned meat loaf with real mashed potatoes. **Known for:** fresh seafood; busy spot requiring reservations; amazing foccacia. $ *Average main: $36* ⌂ *921 Truman Ave., Old Town* ☎ *305/296–2777* ⊕ *www.7fish. com* ⊙ *Closed Tues. No lunch.*

☕ Coffee and Quick Bites

Croissants de France

$ | FRENCH | Pop into the bakery for something sinfully sweet, or spend some time people-watching at the sidewalk café next door. You can get breakfast or lunch at the café, and the bakery is open late. **Known for:** gluten-free buckwheat crepes; popular with both locals and visitors; great coffee and croissants. $ *Average main: $14* ⌂ *816 Duval St., Old Town* ☎ *305/294–2624* ⊕ *www. croissantsdefrance.com.*

★ La Grignote

$ | FRENCH | FAMILY | This is the place to satisfy any French-pastry craving—from the made-from-scratch croissants to the cookies, muffins, coconut macarons, and of course, breads. A lovely patio is the perfect backdrop for breakfasts of brioche French toast, quiches with fresh salads, and a croque madame oozing with

One of Key West's most beloved places to stay is the Gardens Hotel in Old Town.

bechamel and poached eggs. **Known for:** ham-and-cheese crois-sants; friendly owners; French breakfasts. $ *Average main: $11* ✉ *1211 Duval St., Old Town* ☎ *305/916–5445* ⊕ *lagrignotecafe.com* ⊗ *Closed Mon.*

Hotels

Ambrosia Key West

$$$ | B&B/INN | FAMILY | If you desire personal attention, a casual atmosphere, and a dollop of style, stay at these twin inns spread out on nearly 2 acres. **Pros:** spacious rooms; breakfast served poolside; great location. **Cons:** on-street parking can be tough to come by; a little too spread out; high windows in some rooms let in the early morning light. $ *Rooms from: $385* ✉ *615, 618, 622 Fleming St., Old Town* ☎ *305/296–9838, 800/535–9838* ⊕ *www. ambrosiakeywest.com* ⇱ *20 rooms* ⓞ *Free Breakfast.*

Angelina Guesthouse

$ | B&B/INN | In the heart of Old Town, this adults-only home away from home offers simple, clean, attractively priced accommoda-tions. **Pros:** good value; nice garden; friendly staff. **Cons:** thin walls; basic rooms with no TVs; shared balcony and four of the rooms share a bathroom. $ *Rooms from: $159* ✉ *302 Angela St., Old Town* ☎ *305/294–4480, 888/303–4480* ⊕ *www.angelinaguest-house.com* ⇱ *13 rooms* ⓞ *Free Breakfast.*

Azul Key West

$$ | B&B/INN | The ultramodern, nearly minimalistic redo of this classic, circa-1903 Queen Anne mansion—an adults-only property—offers a break from the sensory overload of Key West's other abundant Victorian guesthouses. **Pros:** lovely building; marble-floored baths; luxurious linens. **Cons:** on a busy street; modern isn't for everyone; staff not on site. ⑤ *Rooms from: $289* ⊠ *907 Truman Ave., Old Town* ☎ *305/296–5152, 888/253–2985* ⊕ *www. dwellkeywest.com/key-west-vacation-rentals/azul* ⇨ *11 rooms* ⑩ *Free Breakfast.*

Casa Marina, Curio Collection by Hilton

$$$ | RESORT | FAMILY | This luxurious property is on the largest private beach in Key West, and it has the same richly appointed lobby with beamed ceilings, polished pine floor, and original art as it did when it opened in 1920 on New Year's Eve. Guest rooms are stylishly decorated in neutral colors that evoke a certain comfortable crispness. **Pros:** huge beach; on-site dining, bars, and water sports; away from the crowds. **Cons:** long walk to central Old Town; expensive resort fee; spa is across the street in a separate building. ⑤ *Rooms from: $399* ⊠ *1500 Reynolds St., Old Town* ☎ *305/296–3535, 866/203–6392* ⊕ *www.casamarinaresort.com* ⇨ *311 rooms* ⑩ *No Meals.*

Crowne Plaza La Concha

$$$ | HOTEL | History and franchises can mix, as this 1920s-vintage hotel proves with its handsome atrium lobby and sleep-conducive rooms. **Pros:** location is everything; good on-site restaurant and wine bar; free Wi-Fi. **Cons:** high-traffic area; rooms are small, bathrooms are smaller; expensive valet-only parking. ⑤ *Rooms from: $350* ⊠ *430 Duval St., Old Town* ☎ *305/296–2991* ⊕ *www. laconchakeywest.com* ⇨ *178 rooms* ⑩ *No Meals.*

Eden House

$$ | HOTEL | From the vintage metal rockers on the street-side porch to the old neon hotel sign in the lobby, this 1920s rambling Key West mainstay hotel is high on character, low on gloss. **Pros:** free parking; hot tub is actually hot; daily happy hour around the pool. **Cons:** pricey for older rooms; brown towels take getting used to; parking is first-come, first-served. ⑤ *Rooms from: $225* ⊠ *1015 Fleming St., Old Town* ☎ *305/296–6868, 800/533–5397* ⊕ *www. edenhouse.com* ⇨ *44 rooms* ⑩ *No Meals.*

★ The Gardens Hotel

$$$$ | HOTEL | Built in 1875, this gloriously shaded property was a labor of love from the get-go, and it covers a third of a city block in Old Town. **Pros:** luxurious bathrooms; secluded garden seating; free Wi-Fi. **Cons:** hard to get reservations; expensive; nightly secure parking fee. $ *Rooms from: $415* ✉ *526 Angela St., Old Town* ☎ *305/294–2661, 800/526–2664* ⊕ *www.gardenshotel.com* ⌐ *20 suites* ⦶ *Free Breakfast.*

The Grand Maloney

$$$ | HOTEL | It took nearly two years to restore this property—dating from the late 19th century and named after Walter C. Maloney, Key West's mayor in 1846—into a chic getaway. **Pros:** 3-minute walk to Duval; modern decor; small enough for an entire group buyout. **Cons:** no front desk staff on site; no dining on site; no reserved parking. $ *Rooms from: $299* ✉ *529 Caroline St., Old Town* ☎ *305/294–3265* ⊕ *www.grandmaloneyhotel.com* ⌐ *6 rooms* ⦶ *No Meals.*

Harborside Motel & Marina

$ | HOTEL | This little motel neatly packages three appealing characteristics—affordability, safety, and a pleasant location between Old Town and New Town at Garrison Bight. **Pros:** grills for cookouts; friendly fishing atmosphere; boat slips for guests. **Cons:** more than a mile from Duval Street; no parking for boat trailers; minimum stays for special events and holidays. $ *Rooms from: $199* ✉ *903 Eisenhower Dr., Old Town* ☎ *305/294–2780, 800/501–7823* ⊕ *www.keywestharborside.com* ⌐ *16 rooms* ⦶ *No Meals.*

H2O Suites

$$$$ | HOTEL | Take the plunge at this swanky, luxurious, adults-only (age 25 and up) hotel, where half the one-bedroom suites have a private plunge pool. **Pros:** on-site garage parking; rooms have the most flattering lighting—ever; beach-chair setup at nearby South Beach. **Cons:** pricey resort fee; smoking is allowed outdoors; long walk to the happening side of Duval Street. $ *Rooms from: $499* ✉ *1212 Simonton St., Old Town* ☎ *305/296–3432* ⊕ *www.h2osuites.com* ⌐ *22 suites* ⦶ *No Meals.*

Island City House Hotel

$$$ | B&B/INN | FAMILY | A private garden with brick walkways, tropical plants, and a canopy of palms sets this convivial guesthouse apart from the pack. **Pros:** lush gardens; knowledgeable staff; bike rentals on site. **Cons:** spotty Wi-Fi service; front desk is staffed only 8 am–8 pm; no parking. $ *Rooms from: $320* ✉ *411 William St., Old Town* ☎ *305/294–5702, 800/634–8230* ⊕ *www.islandcity-house.com* ⌐ *24 suites* ⦶ *No Meals.*

Island House

$$$$ | HOTEL | Geared specifically toward gay men, this hotel features a health club, a video lounge, a café and bar, and rooms in historic digs. **Pros:** lots of privacy; just the place to get that all-over tan; free happy hour for guests. **Cons:** no women allowed; three

rooms share a bath; day passes bring visitors of every age, which is a pro or con depending on your mood. ⓢ *Rooms from: $459* ✉ *1129 Fleming St., Old Town* ☎ *305/294–6284, 800/890–6284* ⊕ *www.islandhousekeywest.com* ⤴ *34 rooms* ❌ *No Meals.*

Key West Bed and Breakfast/The Popular House

$ | B&B/INN | There are accommodations for every budget here, but the owners reason that budget travelers deserve as pleasant an experience (and as lavish a tropical continental breakfast) as their well-heeled counterparts. **Pros:** lots of art; tiled outdoor shower; hot tub and sauna area is a welcome hangout. **Cons:** some rooms are small; four rooms have shared baths; historic homes have thinner walls. ⓢ *Rooms from: $145* ✉ *415 William St., Old Town* ☎ *305/296–7274, 800/438–6155* ⊕ *www.keywestbandb.com* ⤴ *10 rooms* ❌ *Free Breakfast.*

La Pensione

$$ | B&B/INN | Hospitality and period furnishings make this 1891 home, once owned by a cigar executive, a wonderful glimpse into Key West life in the late 19th century. **Pros:** pine-paneled walls; first-come, first-served parking included; some rooms have wrapa-round porches. **Cons:** street-facing rooms are noisy; rooms do not have TVs; rooms accommodate only two people. ⓢ *Rooms from: $258* ✉ *809 Truman Ave., Old Town* ☎ *305/292–9923, 800/893–1193* ⊕ *www.lapensione.com* ⤴ *9 rooms* ❌ *Free Breakfast.*

The Marker

$$$ | RESORT | The Marker is a welcome and luxurious option on the waterfront in Old Town, with conch-style architecture and an authentic Keys aesthetic. **Pros:** convenient Old Town location; large private balconies; three saltwater pools, including one for adults only. **Cons:** hefty resort and parking fees nightly; "locals welcome" policy means pool chairs can be hard to come by; lots of walking if your room isn't near the amenities. ⓢ *Rooms from: $400* ✉ *200 William St., Old Town* ☎ *305/501–5193* ⊕ *www.themarkerkeywest.com* ⤴ *96 rooms* ❌ *No Meals.*

★ Marquesa Hotel

$$$ | HOTEL | In a town that prides itself on its laid-back luxury, this complex of four restored 1884 houses stands out. **Pros:** room service; romantic atmosphere; turndown service. **Cons:** street-facing rooms can be noisy; expensive rates; no elevator. ⓢ *Rooms from: $395* ✉ *600 Fleming St., Old Town* ☎ *305/292–1919, 800/869–4631* ⊕ *www.marquesa.com* ⤴ *27 rooms* ❌ *No Meals* ⚲ *No children under age 14 allowed.*

The Mermaid & the Alligator

$$ | **B&B/INN** | An enchanting combination of flora and fauna makes this 1904 Victorian house a welcoming retreat. **Pros:** hot plunge pool; massage pavilion; island-getaway feel. **Cons:** minimum stay required (length depends on season); dark public areas; plastic lawn chairs. $ *Rooms from: $278* ⊠ *729 Truman Ave., Old Town* ☎ *305/294–1894, 800/773–1894* ⊕ *www.kwmermaid.com* ➟ *9 rooms* �‡ *Free Breakfast.*

NYAH: Not Your Average Hotel

$$$ | **B&B/INN** | From its charming white picket fence, it may look similar to other Victorian-style Key West B&Bs, but that's where the similarities end, as this adults-only property's minimalistic rooms (all with upscale, private baths) have customizable sleeping arrangements: up to six can stay in one room, and all get their own bed. **Pros:** central location; perfect for traveling with a group of friends; free daily happy hour. **Cons:** small rooms, even smaller closets; street parking only; no toiletries provided. $ *Rooms from: $349* ⊠ *420 Margaret St., Old Town* ☎ *305/296–2131* ⊕ *www. nyahotels.com* ➟ *36 rooms* ❑ *Free Breakfast* ☞ *Age 18 and over only.*

★ Ocean Key Resort & Spa

$$$$ | **RESORT** | This full resort—relatively rare in Key West—has large, tropical-look rooms and excellent on-site amenities, including a pool and bar overlooking Sunset Pier and a Thai-inspired spa. **Pros:** well-trained staff; lively pool scene; fantastic location at the busy end of Duval. **Cons:** daily valet parking and resort fee; too bustling for some; rooms are starting to show their age. $ *Rooms from: $495* ⊠ *0 Duval St., Old Town* ☎ *305/296–7701, 800/328–9815* ⊕ *www.oceankey.com* ➟ *100 rooms* ❑ *No Meals.*

Opal Key Resort & Marina

$$$$ | **RESORT** | **FAMILY** | This waterfront resort's two three-story, Keys-style buildings huddle around its 37-slip marina in the middle of Old Town overlooking Mallory Square. **Pros:** location in the heart of Old Town; bottled water and other useful amenities in room; valet parking in its garage. **Cons:** pricey; small pool for such a huge place; hefty parking and resort fees. $ *Rooms from: $425* ⊠ *245 Front St., Old Town* ☎ *305/294–4000* ⊕ *www.opalcollection.com/ opal-key* ➟ *210 rooms* ❑ *No Meals.*

Pier House Resort & Spa

$$$$ | **RESORT** | This upscale resort, near Mallory Square in the heart of Old Town, offers a wide range of amenities, including a beach and comfortable, traditionally furnished rooms. **Pros:** beautiful beach; free Wi-Fi; nice spa and restaurant. **Cons:** lots of conventions; poolside rooms are small; not really suitable for children under 16. *$ Rooms from: $470 ✉ 1 Duval St., Old Town ☎ 305/296–4600, 800/327–8340 🌐 www.pierhouse.com 145 rooms 🍴 No Meals.*

The Reach Key West, Curio Collection by Hilton
$$$ | **RESORT** | **FAMILY** | Embracing Key West's only natural beach, this full-service, luxury resort offers stylish rooms—all with balconies and modern amenities—and access to the spa, pools, and other facilities at the nearby Casa Marina resort. **Pros:** removed from Duval hubbub; great sunrise views; pullout sofas in most rooms. **Cons:** expensive resort fee; high rates; lacks the grandeur you'd expect of a resort property. *$ Rooms from: $399 ✉ 1435 Simonton St., Old Town ☎ 305/296–5000, 888/318–4316 🌐 www.reachresort.com 150 rooms 🍴 No Meals.*

★ Santa Maria Suites
$$$$ | **RESORT** | It's odd to call this a hidden gem when it sits on a prominent corner just one block off Duval, but a concrete facade keeps this luxurious find well secluded from the outside world. **Pros:** amenities galore; front desk concierge services; private parking lot. **Cons:** daily resort fee; poolside units must close curtains for privacy; only two-bedroom units available. *$ Rooms from: $549 ✉ 1401 Simonton St., Old Town ☎ 866/726–8259, 305/296–5678 🌐 www.santamariasuites.com 35 suites 🍴 No Meals.*

Simonton Court
$$$ | **B&B/INN** | A small world all its own, this adults-only maze of accommodations and four swimming pools makes you feel deliciously sequestered from Key West's crasser side but keeps you close enough to get there on foot. **Pros:** lots of privacy; well-appointed accommodations; friendly staff. **Cons:** minimum stay required in high season; off-street parking $25 nightly; some street noise in basic rooms. *$ Rooms from: $310 ✉ 320 Simonton St., Old Town ☎ 305/294–6386, 800/944–2687 🌐 www.simontoncourt.com 29 rooms 🍴 Free Breakfast.*

★ Southernmost Beach Resort
$$$ | **HOTEL** | **FAMILY** | Rooms at this hotel on the quiet end of Duval—a 20-minute walk from downtown—are modern and sophisticated, and although the area around it gets some car and foot traffic, the property is far enough from the hubbub that you can relax but close enough that you can participate if you wish. **Pros:** pool attracts a lively crowd; access to nearby properties and beach; free Wi-Fi. **Cons:** can get crowded around the pool and public areas; expensive nightly resort fee; beach is across the street. *$ Rooms from: $359 ✉ 1319 Duval St., Old Town ☎ 305/296–6577, 800/354–4455 🌐 www.southernmostbeachresort.com 118 rooms 🍴 No Meals.*

Southwinds Motel

$$ | B&B/INN | Operated by the same company as the ultra-high-end Santa Maria Suites, this motel-style property is a good-value option in pricey Key West. **Pros:** early (2 pm) check-in may be available; spacious rooms; free parking and Wi-Fi. **Cons:** bland decor; small pools; thin walls. $ *Rooms from: $200 ⊠ 1321 Simonton St., Old Town* ☎ *305/296–2829, 877/879–2362* ⊕ *www.keywest-southwinds.com* ⇥ *58 rooms* ⦿ *Free Breakfast.*

Speakeasy Inn

$ | B&B/INN | During Prohibition, Raul Vasquez made this place popular by smuggling in rum from Cuba; today, its reputation is for having reasonably priced rooms within walking distance of the beach. **Pros:** good location; all rooms have kitchenettes; first-come, first-served free parking. **Cons:** no pool; on busy Duval; rooms are fairly basic. $ *Rooms from: $189 ⊠ 1117 Duval St., Old Town* ☎ *305/296–2680* ⊕ *www.speakeasyinn.com* ⇥ *7 suites* ⦿ *Free Breakfast.*

★ Sunset Key Cottages

$$$$ | RESORT | FAMILY | This luxurious, private-island retreat with its own beach feels completely cut off from the world, yet it's just a 10-minute ride—via a free, 24-hour ferry—from the action in Mallory Square. **Pros:** all units have kitchens; roomy verandas; excellent Latitudes restaurant. **Cons:** luxury doesn't come cheap; beach shore is rocky; launch runs only every 30 minutes. $ *Rooms from: $780 ⊠ 245 Front St., Old Town* ☎ *305/292–5300, 888/477–7786* ⊕ *www.opalcollection.com/sunset-key-cottages* ⇥ *40 cottages* ⦿ *Free Breakfast.*

Westwinds Inn

$$ | B&B/INN | This cluster of historic gingerbread-trimmed houses has individually decorated, homey rooms with muted tropical colors and simple furnishings. **Pros:** away from Old Town's bustle; lots of character; affordable rates. **Cons:** small lobby; confusing layout; a long walk from Duval Street. $ *Rooms from: $210 ⊠ 914 Eaton St., Old Town* ☎ *305/296–4440, 800/788–4150* ⊕ *www. westwindskeywest.com* ⇥ *26 rooms* ⦿ *Free Breakfast.*

Winslow's Bungalows

$$$ | HOTEL | Part of the Kimpton Hotel brand, this 1854, Grand Bahama–style house on the National Register of Historic Places is in the center of Key West, just two blocks off Duval Street, and features vibrant gardens, three private pools, and an outdoor bar. **Pros:** walking distance to clubs and bars; some rooms have private outdoor spaces; free Wi-Fi. **Cons:** over a mile to the sunset end of Duval Street; pool faces a busy street; $20 daily parking fee. $ *Rooms from: $359 ⊠ 725 Truman Ave., Old*

Town ☎ *305/294–5229, 800/549–4430* ⊕ *www.kimptonkeywest. com/key-west-hotels/winslows-bungalows* ⇥ *85 rooms* ⚫ *Free Breakfast.*

Nightlife

BARS AND LOUNGES

Aqua

BARS | Key West's largest gay bar, Aqua hosts karaoke contests, dancing, and live entertainment at three bars, including one outside on the patio. For an evening like no other, come see the Aquanettes at their "Reality Is a Drag" show. ⊠ *711 Duval St., Old Town* ☎ *305/294–0555* ⊕ *www.aquakeywest.com.*

★ Capt. Tony's Saloon

BARS | When it was the original Sloppy Joe's in the mid-1930s, Hemingway was a regular. Later, a young Jimmy Buffett sang here and made this watering hole famous in his song "Last Mango in Paris." Captain Tony was even voted mayor of Key West. Yes, this place is a beloved landmark. Stop in and take a look at the "hanging tree" that grows through the roof, listen to live music seven nights a week, and play some pool. ⊠ *428 Greene St., Old Town* ☎ *305/294–1838* ⊕ *www.capttonyssaloon.com.*

Durty Harry's

BARS | This megasize entertainment complex is home to eight different bars and clubs, both indoor and outdoor. Their motto is "Eight Famous Bars, One Awesome Night," and they're right. You'll find pizza, dancing, live music, Rick's Key West, and the infamous Red Garter strip club. ⊠ *208 Duval St., Old Town* ☎ *305/296–5513* ⊕ *www.facebook.com/rickskeywest.*

Garden of Eden

BARS | Perhaps one of Duval's more unusual and intriguing watering holes, the Garden of Eden sits atop the Bull & Whistle saloon and has a clothing-optional policy. Most drinkers are lookie-loos, but some actually bare it all, including the barmaids. ⊠ *224 Duval St., Old Town* ☎ *305/396–4565* ⊕ *bullkeywest.com/garden-of-eden.*

★ Green Parrot Bar

BARS | Pause for a libation in the open air and breathe in the spirit of Key West. Built in 1890 as a grocery store, this property has been many things to many people over the years. It's touted as the oldest bar in Key West, and the sometimes rowdy saloon has locals outnumbering out-of-towners, especially on nights when bands play. ⊠ *601 Whitehead St., at Southard St., Old Town* ☎ *305/294–6133* ⊕ *www.greenparrot.com.*

Island House Bar & Café

BARS | Part of a men's resort, Island House Bar & Café serves frozen and other cocktails along with creative cuisine in tropical gardens with a pool where clothing is optional. It is open 24 hours. ⊠ *Island House, 1129 Fleming St., Old Town* ☎ *305/294–6284, 800/890–6284* ⊕ *www.islandhousekeywest.com.*

Mangoes

BARS | On a busy corner right on bustling Duval Street, it's the perfect spot for people-watching and being part of the action. Find a seat at the bar, especially at happy hour, for half-price appetizers and drink deals. ⊠ *700 Duval St., corner of Angela St., Old Town* ☎ *305/294–8002* ⊕ *www.mangoeskeywest.com.*

Pier House

BARS | The party begins at the Beach Bar, with live entertainment daily to celebrate sunset on the beach, and then moves to the Chart Room. It's small and odd, but there are free hot dogs and peanuts, and its history is intriguing. ⊠ *1 Duval St., Old Town* ☎ *305/296–4600, 800/327–8340* ⊕ *www.pierhouse.com.*

Schooner Wharf Bar

BARS | This open-air waterfront bar and grill retains its funky Key West charm and hosts live entertainment daily. Its margaritas rank among Key West's best, as does the bar itself, voted Best Local's Bar six years in a row. For great views, head up to the second floor and be sure to order up some fresh seafood and fritters and Dark and Stormy cocktails. ⊠ *202 William St., Old Town* ☎ *305/292–3302* ⊕ *www.schoonerwharf.com.*

★ Sloppy Joe's

BARS | There's history and good times at the successor to a famous 1937 speakeasy named for its founder, Captain Joe Russell. Decorated with Hemingway memorabilia and marine flags, the bar is full and noisy all the time. A Sloppy Joe's T-shirt is a de rigueur Key West souvenir, and the gift shop sells them like crazy. Grab a seat (if you can), and be entertained by the bands—and the parade of people in constant motion. ⊠ *201 Duval St., Old Town* ☎ *305/294–5717* ⊕ *www.sloppyjoes.com.*

Two Friends Patio Lounge

BARS | Love karaoke? Get it out of your system at Two Friends Patio Lounge, where your performance gets a live Internet feed via the bar's Karaoke Cam. The singing starts at 8:30 most nights. The Bloody Marys are famous. ⊠ *512 Front St., Old Town* ☎ *305/296–3124* ⊕ *www.twofriends.com.*

CABARETS
La Te Da Hotel and Bar
CABARET | This venue hosts female impersonators (catch Christopher Peterson when he's on stage) and riotously funny cabaret shows nightly in the Crystal Room Cabaret Lounge. There is also live entertainment nightly, featuring a variety of local stars, including the ever-popular Debra in the ultracool Piano Bar. ⊠ *1125 Duval St., Old Town* ☎ *305/296–6706* ⊕ *www.lateda.com.*

DANCE CLUBS
Bourbon Street Complex
DANCE CLUBS | Pick your entertainment at the Bourbon Street Complex, a club within an all-male guesthouse. There are 10 video screens along with dancers grooving to the latest music spun by DJs at the Bourbon Street Pub. ⊠ *724 Duval St., Old Town* ☎ *305/293–9800* ⊕ *www.bourbonstpub.com.*

LIVE MUSIC
Hog's Breath Saloon
LIVE MUSIC | Belly up to the bar for a cold mug of the signature Hog's Breath Lager at this infamous joint, a must-stop on the Key West bar crawl. Live bands play daily 1 pm–2 am (except when the game's on TV). You never know who'll stop by and perhaps even jump on stage for an impromptu concert (can you say Kenny Chesney?). ⊠ *400 Front St., Old Town* ☎ *305/296–4222* ⊕ *www. hogsbreath.com.*

Margaritaville
LIVE MUSIC | A youngish, touristy crowd mixes with aging Parrot Heads. It's owned by former Key West resident and recording star Jimmy Buffett, who has been known to perform here. The drink of choice is, of course, a margarita, made with Jimmy's own brand of Margaritaville tequila. There's live music nightly, as well as lunch and dinner. ⊠ *500 Duval St., Old Town* ☎ *305/292–1435* ⊕ *www. margaritavillekeywest.com.*

🎭 Performing Arts

Red Barn Theatre
THEATER | Since the 1980s, the Red Barn Theatre, a small professional theater company, has performed dramas, comedies, and musicals, including works by new playwrights. Big things happen in this little theater, and it's well worth a visit while you're here. ⊠ *319 Duval St. (rear), Old Town* ☎ *305/296–9911, 866/870–9911* ⊕ *www.redbarntheatre.com.*

South Florida Symphony Orchestra

MUSIC | Key West native and nationally recognized conductor Sebrina María Alfonso directs the South Florida Symphony Orchestra (formerly the Key West Symphony Orchestra). This traveling group of symphonic musicians is based in Fort Lauderdale and performs at the Glynn R. Archer Center for the Performing Arts while in Key West. ⊠ *Old Town* ☎ *954/522–8445* ⊕ *www.southfloridasymphony.org.*

Tropic Cinema

FILM | Catch the classics and the latest art, independent, and foreign films shown daily in this four-screen theater. A full-concession café with beer and wine is available. This is *the* place to catch a show in Key West. ⊠ *416 Eaton St., Old Town* ☎ *305/294–5857, 877/761–3456* ⊕ *www.tropiccinema.com.*

Waterfront Playhouse

THEATER | Home to the Key West Players, this community-run, 180-seat playhouse—in a converted, 1880s ice warehouse—presents comedy and drama from December to May. The troupe first banded together in 1940, counting Tennessee Williams among its members. ⊠ *Mallory Sq., Old Town* ☎ *305/294–5015* ⊕ *www. waterfrontplayhouse.org.*

Shopping

ARTS AND CRAFTS

Local artists do a great job of preserving the island's architecture and spirit, so Key West is filled with art galleries—many along the south end of Duval Street—and the variety is truly amazing. Although local artists are well represented, many galleries carry works by international artists as well.

Alan S. Maltz Gallery

ART GALLERIES | The owner, declared the state's official wildlife photographer by the Fish & Wildlife Foundation of Florida, captures the state's nature and character in stunning portraits. Spend four figures for large-format images on canvas or save on small prints and closeouts. ⊠ *1210 Duval St., Old Town* ☎ *305/294–0005* ⊕ *www.alanmaltz.com.*

Art at 830

ART GALLERIES | This inviting gallery carries a little bit of everything, from pottery to paintings and jewelry to sculptures. Most outstanding is its selection of glass art, particularly the jellyfish lamps. Take time to admire all that is here. ⊠ *830 Caroline St., Old Town* ☎ *305/295–9595* ⊕ *www.art830.com.*

Gallery on Greene

ART GALLERIES | This is the largest gallery–exhibition space in Key West, and it showcases 37 museum-quality artists. It prides itself on being the leader in the field of representational fine art, painting, sculptures, and reproductions from the Florida Keys and Key West. You can see the love immediately from gallery curator Nancy Frank, who aims to please everyone, from the casual buyer to the established collector. ⊠ *606 Greene St., Old Town* ☎ *305/294–1669* ⊕ *www.galleryongreene.com.*

Gingerbread Square Gallery

ART GALLERIES | The oldest private art gallery in Key West represents local and internationally acclaimed artists on an annually changing basis, in media ranging from paintings to art glass. ⊠ *1207 Duval St., Old Town* ☎ *305/296–8900* ⊕ *www.ginger-breadsquaregallery.com.*

Key West Pottery

CERAMICS | You won't find any painted coconuts here, but you will find a collection of contemporary tropical ceramics. Wife-and-husband owners Kelly Lever and Adam Russell take real pride in this working studio that, in addition to their own creations, features artists from around the country. ⊠ *1203 Duval St., Old Town* ☎ *305/900–8303* ⊕ *www.keywestpottery.com.*

★ Wyland Gallery

ART GALLERIES | Painter, sculptor, and photographer Robert Wyland is world renowned for his marine-life art pieces and conservation efforts. You'll get your first glimpse of his work as you enter the Keys: he chose the Bimini Blue paint for the concrete safety walls that stretch from the mainland to Key Largo. At Mile Marker 99.2, you can't miss *Keys to the Seas,* one of his famed "whaling wall" murals; *Florida's Radiant Reef* is in Marathon, at Mile Marker 55.5; *Florida's Living Reef* is in Key West at the foot of William Street (Guy Harvey helped on this one). This gallery carries many incredible works by Wyland and other marine-life artists. You might not be able to afford anything, but viewing the art is the equivalent of exploring underwater without getting your hair wet. ⊠ *623 Duval St., Old Town* ☎ *305/292–4998* ⊕ *www.wylandgalleriesofthefloridakeys.com.*

BOOKS

★ Books & Books @ The Studios of Key West

BOOKS | FAMILY | This nonprofit, independently minded, neighborhood bookstore is the brainchild of a small group of local booklovers, led by authors and Key West residents Judy Blume and her husband George Cooper. It is affiliated with the Miami-based book store of the same name and is in The Studios of Key West, a nonprofit arts center providing artist-in-residency opportunities for artists and writers. If you stop by, you might find Judy behind the register or stocking books. ⊠ *533 Eaton St., Historic Seaport* ☎ *305/320–0208* ⊕ *booksandbookskw.com.*

Key West Island Bookstore

This home away from home for the large Key West writers' community carries new, used, and rare titles. It specializes in Hemingway, Tennessee Williams, and South Florida mystery writers. ⊠ *513 Fleming St., Old Town* ☎ *305/294–2904* ⊕ *www. keywestislandbooks.com.*

CLOTHING AND FABRICS

Fairvilla Megastore

OTHER SPECIALTY STORE | Don't leave town without a browse through the legendary shop. Although it's not really a clothing store, you'll find an astonishing array of fantasy wear and outlandish costumes (check out the pirate section), as well as other "adult" toys. (Some of the products may make you blush.) ⊠ *520 Front St., Old Town* ☎ *305/292–0448* ⊕ *www.fairvilla.com.*

★ Kino Sandals

SHOES | A pair of Kino sandals was once a public declaration that you'd been to Key West. The attraction? You can watch these inexpensive items being made. The factory has been churning out several styles since 1966. Walk up to the counter, grab a pair, try them on, and lay down some cash. It's that simple. ⊠ *107 Fitzpatrick St., Old Town* ☎ *305/294–5044* ⊕ *www.kinosandalfactory.com.*

The Seam Shoppe

FABRICS | Take home a shopping bag full of scarlet hibiscus, fuchsia heliconia, blue parrotfish, and even pink flamingo fabric chosen from the city's widest selection of tropical-print fabrics. ⊠ *1113 Truman Ave., Old Town* ☎ *305/296–9830* ⊕ *www.tropicalfabricsonline.com.*

FOOD AND DRINK

Fausto's Food Palace

FOOD | Since 1926 Fausto's has been the spot to catch up on the week's gossip and to chill out in summer—it has groceries, organic foods, marvelous wines, a sushi chef on duty 8 am–3 pm, and box lunches and dinners-by-the-pound to go. There are two locations you can shop at in Key West (the other is at 1105 White Street) plus an online store. ⊠ *522 Fleming St., Old Town* ☎ *305/296–5663* ⊕ *www.faustos.com.*

★ Kermit's Key West Key Lime Shoppe

FOOD | You'll see Kermit himself standing on the corner every time a trolley passes, pie in hand. He carries many key lime products—from barbecue sauce to jelly beans—and his key lime pie is the best on the island. Once you try it, perhaps frozen on a stick and dipped in chocolate, you may consider quitting your job and moving here. Savor every bite in the patio-garden area, or come for breakfast or lunch in the on-site café. Note, too, that Kermit's frozen pies, topped with a special long-lasting whipped cream instead of meringue, travel well. There's a smaller second location on the corner of Duval and Front Streets. ✉ *200 Elizabeth St., Old Town* ☎ *305/296–0806, 800/376–0806* ⊕ *www.keylimeshop.com.*

GIFTS AND SOUVENIRS

Cayo Hueso y Habana Historeum

SOUVENIRS | Part museum, part shopping center, this circa-1879 warehouse includes a hand-rolled-cigar shop, one-of-a-kind souvenirs, a Cuban restaurant, and exhibits that tell of the island's Cuban heritage. Outside, a memorial garden pays homage to the island's Cuban ancestors. ✉ *Mallory Sq., 410 Wall St., Old Town* ☎ *305/293–7260.*

HEALTH AND BEAUTY

★ Key West Aloe

SKINCARE | This shop produces hundreds of soap, candle, sunscreen, and skin-care products for men and women. Soothe your skin from head to toe and slather on natural, tropical products that boast an added boost from science. A second location is at 1075 Duval. ✉ *416 Greene St., at Simonton St., Old Town* ☎ *305/735–4927, 800/445–2563* ⊕ *www.keywestaloe.com.*

SHOPPING CENTERS

Bahama Village

SHOPPING CENTER | Where to start your shopping adventure? This cluster of spruced-up shops, restaurants, and vendors is responsible for the restoration of the colorful historic district where Bahamians settled in the 19th century. The village lies roughly between Whitehead and Fort Streets and Angela and Catherine Streets. Hemingway frequented the bars, restaurants, and boxing rings in this part of town. ✉ *Old Town* ✛ *Between Whitehead and Fort Sts. and Angela and Catherine Sts.*

The Conch Republic

Beginning in the 1970s, pot smuggling became a source of income for islanders who knew how to dodge detection in the maze of waterways in the Keys. In 1982, the U.S. Border Patrol threw a roadblock across the Overseas Highway just south of Florida City to catch drug runners and undocumented aliens. Traffic backed up for miles as Border Patrol agents searched vehicles and demanded that the occupants prove U.S. citizenship.

Officials in Key West, outraged at being treated like foreigners by the federal government, staged a protest and formed their own "nation," the so-called Conch Republic. They hoisted a flag and distributed mock border passes, visas, and Conch currency. The embarrassed Border Patrol dismantled its roadblock, and now an annual festival recalls the city's victory.

New Town

The Overseas Highway splits as it enters Key West, the two forks rejoining to encircle New Town, the area east of White Street to Cow Key Channel. The southern fork runs along the shore as South Roosevelt Boulevard (Route A1A) and skirts Key West International Airport, while the northern fork runs along the north shore as North Roosevelt Boulevard and turns into Truman Avenue once it hits Old Town. Part of New Town was created with dredged fill. The island would have continued growing this way had the Army Corps of Engineers not determined in the early 1970s that it was detrimental to the nearby reef.

TIMING

If your interests lie in art, gardens, or Civil War history, allow three or four hours to visit the Fort East Martello Museum and Gardens. Throw in lunch and time at the beach and make it a full-day affair.

Sights

Fort East Martello Museum and Gardens

ART MUSEUM | This redbrick Civil War fort never saw a lick of action during the war. Today it serves as a museum, operated by the Key West Art & Historical Society, with exhibits about the 19th and 20th centuries, including relics from the USS *Maine,* cigar factory and shipwrecking displays, and a collection of Stanley Papio's "junk art" sculptures and Cuban folk artist Mario Sanchez's chiseled and painted wooden carvings of historic Key West street scenes. You can climb to the top of the citadel tower. ⊠ *3501 S. Roosevelt Blvd., New Town* ☎ *305/296–3913* ⊕ *www.kwahs.com* ⊠ *$16.*

Beaches

Rest Beach/C. B. Harvey Memorial Park
BEACH | This beach and park were named after Cornelius Bradford Harvey, former Key West mayor and commissioner. Adjacent to Higgs Beach, it has half a dozen picnic areas across the street, dunes, a pier, and a wheelchair and bike path. **Amenities:** none. **Best for:** walking. ⊠ *Atlantic Blvd., east side of White St. Pier, New Town* ⊠ *Free.*

★ Smathers Beach
BEACH | This wide beach has nearly 1 mile of nice white sand, plus beautiful coconut palms, picnic areas, and volleyball courts, all of which make it popular with the spring-break crowd. Trucks along the road rent rafts, windsurfers, and other beach "toys." **Amenities:** food and drink; parking; toilets; water sports. **Best for:** partiers. ⊠ *S. Roosevelt Blvd., New Town* ⊠ *Free.*

 Restaurants

Tavern N Town
$$$ | **ECLECTIC** | At this handsome restaurant, lovely aromas waft from the wood-fired oven in the open kitchen. Among the popular choices on the dinner menu, which has both small plates and full entrées, are lemon-crusted sea scallops, rack of Colorado lamb, and small pizzas (including a white seafood version). **Known for:** upscale atmosphere (and prices); popular happy hour; noise when busy. ⓢ *Average main: $33* ⊠ *Key West Marriott Beachside Resort, 3841 N. Roosevelt Blvd., New Town* ☎ *305/296–8100, 800/546–0885* ⊕ *www.tavernntown.com* ☯ *No lunch.*

Hotels

Hampton Inn Key West
$ | **HOTEL** | **FAMILY** | You know what to expect from this chain hotel: well-maintained rooms, predictable service, and competitive prices. **Pros:** big pool area; popular tiki bar serves liquor and food; free breakfast. **Cons:** roar of airplanes from nearby airport; limited restaurant hours; far from Duval Street. ⓢ *Rooms from: $160* ⊠ *3755*

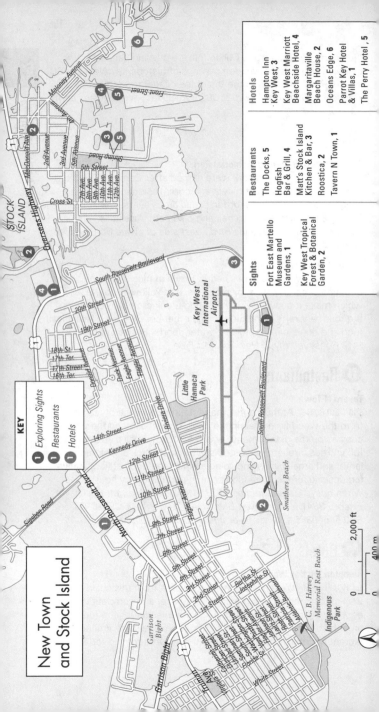

New Town and Stock Island

KEY

- **1** Exploring Sights
- **1** Restaurants
- **1** Hotels

Sights

Fort East Martello Museum and Gardens, **1**

Key West Tropical Forest & Botanical Garden, **2**

Restaurants

The Docks, **5**

Hogfish Bar & Grill, **4**

Matt's Stock Island Kitchen & Bar, **3**

Roostica, **2**

Tavern N Town, **1**

Hotels

Hampton Inn Key West, **3**

Key West Marriott Beachside Hotel, **4**

Margaritaville Beach House, **2**

Oceans Edge, **6**

Parrot Key Hotel & Villas, **1**

The Perry Hotel, **5**

STOCK ISLAND

Maloney Avenue

Front Street

4th Avenue

MacDonald Ave.

2nd Avenue

3rd Avenue

5th Avenue

Sump Road

5th Street

7th Ave.

8th Ave.

9th Ave.

10th Ave.

11th Ave.

12th Ave.

Cross St.

Overseas Highway

South Roosevelt Boulevard

Key West International Airport

South Roosevelt Boulevard

20th Street

19th Street

18th St.

17th Ter.

17th Street

16th Ter.

Duval Avenue

Duck Avenue

Eagle Avenue

Flagler Avenue

Little Hamaca Park

Riviera Drive

14th Street

Kennedy Drive

12th Street

11th Street

10th Street

Smathers Beach

North Roosevelt Blvd.

Sigsbee Road

8th Street

6th Street

5th Street

4th Street

3rd Street

2nd Street

1st Street

Bertha St.

Josephine St.

Garrison Bight

Garrison Bight

C. B. Harvey Memorial Rest Beach

Indigenous Park

Trumbo Ave.

Truman Ave.

White Street

2,000 ft

0

0

400 m

S. Roosevelt Blvd., New Town ☎ *305/296–3500, 800/432–4315* ⊕ *www.hilton.com* ⇱ *100 rooms* ¶Ol *Free Breakfast.*

Key West Marriott Beachside Hotel

$$$$ | HOTEL | FAMILY | This hotel attracts convention business by offering the biggest ballroom in Key West, but it also appeals to families with its spacious, impeccably and tastefully decorated rooms and one-, two-, or three-bedroom condo units. **Pros:** private tanning beach; poolside cabanas; complimentary shuttle to Old Town and airport. **Cons:** no swimming at its beach; lots of conventions and conferences; cookie cutter facade. Ⓢ *Rooms from: $409* ✉ *3841 N. Roosevelt Blvd., New Town* ☎ *305/296–8100, 800/546–0885* ⊕ *www.keywestmarriottbeachside.com* ⇱ *258 units* ¶Ol *No Meals.*

★ Margaritaville Beach House

$$ | RESORT | FAMILY | This property, which definitely has a modern-beach-house feel, features a lagoon-style pool with a waterfall; lush landscaping with pathways, hammocks, and lawn games; and Jimmy Buffet–inspired flair with poolside entertainment and colorful artwork. **Pros:** friendly staff; complimentary cocktail at check-in; all rooms have kitchenettes. **Cons:** not directly on beach; not all rooms have balconies; hefty daily resort fee. Ⓢ *Rooms from: $220* ✉ *2001 S. Roosevelt Blvd., New Town* ☎ *305/292–9800* ⊕ *www.margaritavilleresorts.com/margaritaville-beach-house-key-west* ⇱ *184 rooms* ¶Ol *No Meals.*

Parrot Key Hotel & Villas

$$$ | HOTEL | Rooms here have a crisp, modern look—with beach-cottage chic decor and upbeat pastel color schemes—but this property maintains its old-fashioned beach community feel with picket fences and rocking-chair porches. **Pros:** four pools; finely appointed units; patio, porch, or balcony with all rooms. **Cons:** not within walking distance to Old Town; valet only; hefty resort fee. Ⓢ *Rooms from: $339* ✉ *2801 N. Roosevelt Blvd., New Town* ☎ *305/809–2200* ⊕ *www.parrotkeyresort.com* ⇱ *148 rooms* ¶Ol *No Meals.*

Stock Island

Locals refer to Stock Island as "Old Key West" because parts of it reflect the way the island was before tourism took over. You'll find marinas and working shipyards and waterfronts, the last of their kind, for shrimpers, lobstermen, and commercial fishermen. You'll spy some boatbuilding workshops as well. A laid-back vintage vibe, a monthly art stroll that showcases the island's artists and galleries, two of Key West's newer hotels, and a legendary fish saloon that's a destination in itself all make this under-the-radar spot well worth a visit.

TIMING

You could easily do a weekend getaway here and not bother with venturing into the typical Key West fray. Or pop in for a few hours to see the marinas and get the lay of the land.

Sights

Key West Tropical Forest & Botanical Garden

GARDEN | Established in 1935, this unique habitat is the only frost-free botanical garden in the continental United States. You won't see fancy topiaries and exotic plants, but you will see an ecosystem that is unique to this area and the Caribbean. Paved walkways take you past butterfly gardens, mangroves, Cuban palms, and ponds where you can spy turtles and fish. There are herons, ibis, and other birds here, too. It's a natural slice of Keys paradise that offers a nice respite from sidewalks and shops. ⊠ *5210 College Rd., Stock Island* ☎ *305/296–1504* ⊕ *www.kwbgs.org* 🖾 *$10.*

 Restaurants

★ The Docks

$$$ | **SEAFOOD** | **FAMILY** | This restaurant with views of Stock Island's working marina features fresh, sustainably sourced seafood—from the dining room, you can even watch bivalves being plated on ice in a glass-enclosed oyster-shucking station. A rustic-upcycled, island-style decor belies such sophisticated dishes as the snapper "Philly" sandwich, fresh-off-the-boat ceviche specials, and made-to-order *zeppoles* (cream-, custard-, or jelly-filled fritters) for dessert. **Known for:** friendly service; great wine list; super-fresh seafood. ⑤ *Average main: $27* ⊠ *6840 Front St., Stock Island* ☎ *305/396–7049* ⊕ *thedocksstockisland.com.*

Hogfish Bar & Grill

$ | **SEAFOOD** | It's worth a drive to Stock Island for a meal at this down-to-earth spot, where hogfish is, of course, the specialty. Favorites include the "Killer Hogfish Sandwich," which is served on Cuban bread (be sure to sprinkle it with one of the house hot sauces), as well as the hogfish tacos, gator bites, lobster BLT or pot pie, pulled-pork sandwich, and barbecued ribs. **Known for:** pricey fish sandwiches; a taste of local life; fried grouper cheeks. ⑤ *Average main: $17* ⊠ *6810 Front St., Stock Island* ☎ *305/293–4041* ⊕ *www.hogfishbar.com.*

★ Matt's Stock Island Kitchen & Bar

$$ | **SEAFOOD** | This casual-yet-stylish haven of "American coastal comfort food" has garnered local and national accolades for its eclectic seafood-focused menu and industrial-cool design. The crab beignets are a must, as is the Southern-style fried chicken with bacon salt fries and barbecue ribs. **Known for:** fresh catch of the day; marina views; sophisticated seafood dishes. $ *Average main: $24* ⊠ *Perry Hotel, 7001 Shrimp Rd., Stock Island* ☎ *305/294–3939* ⊕ *www.perrykeywest.com.*

Roostica

$ | **PIZZA** | Neapolitan pizza purists will be impressed with the thin-crust, artisanal pies, all cooked in a wood-burning oven and made with Italian plum tomatoes, mozzarella *di bufala,* and extra-virgin olive oil. And this neighborhood spot, created by the same folks who own the popular Hogfish restaurant, has garnered attention not only for its pizza, but also its Italian comfort food like the spaghetti and meatballs topped with Sunday gravy or the baked lasagna to go; at happy hour, be sure to try the limoncello wood-fired wings. **Known for:** gourmet pizza and nightly specials; friendly service; a bevy of craft beers. $ *Average main: $18* ⊠ *5620 MacDonald Ave., Stock Island* ☎ *305/296–4999* ⊕ *www.roostica.com.*

 ## Hotels

★ Oceans Edge

$$ | **HOTEL** | **FAMILY** | Set on 20 acres, this luxury resort unfurls along a marina with both Atlantic and Gulf views. **Pros:** all rooms have waterfront views; suites include kitchenettes; complimentary shuttle bus to downtown. **Cons:** not walking distance to Old Town; not near a beach; only one restaurant on site. $ *Rooms from: $230* ⊠ *5950 Peninsular Ave., Stock Island* ☎ *305/809–8204* ⊕ *www.oceansedgekeywest.com* ⇥ *175 rooms* ⏉ *No Meals.*

The Perry Hotel

$ | **HOTEL** | This industrial-chic stunner—where spacious, airy rooms juxtapose crisp white linens with furnishings and fixtures in rich chocolate-browns and shades of gray—has made off-the-beaten-path Stock Island a Key West destination. **Pros:** free shuttle to Old Town; direct access to fishing; home to a sophisticated restaurant. **Cons:** 5 miles from Duval Street; limited number of suites; marina slip owners have access to the pool. $ *Rooms from: $170* ⊠ *7001 Shrimp Rd., Stock Island* ☎ *305/296–1717* ⊕ *www. perrykeywest.com* ⇥ *100 rooms* ⏉ *No Meals.*

 Performing Arts

Tennessee Williams Theatre

THEATER | This theater hosts a variety of performing arts events, including chamber music and jazz concerts, dance performances, dramatic plays, and musicals with major stars. ⊠ *Florida Keys Community College, 5901 College Rd., Stock Island* ☎ *305/296–1520 administration, 305/295–7676 box office* ⊕ *twstages.com.*

Activities

Unlike the rest of the region, Key West isn't known primarily for outdoor pursuits. But everyone should devote at least half a day to relaxing on a boat tour, heading out on a fishing expedition, or pursuing some other adventure at sea. The ultimate excursion is a boat or seaplane trip to Dry Tortugas National Park for snorkeling and exploring Fort Jefferson.

Other excursions cater to nature lovers, scuba divers, snorkelers, and folks who just want to get out in or on the water and enjoy the scenery and sunset. For those who prefer land-based recreation, biking is the way to go. Hiking is limited, but walking the streets of Old Town provides plenty of exercise.

Biking

A&M Rentals

BIKING | **FAMILY** | This outfit rents beach cruisers with large baskets, scooters, and electric minicars and has a second location on South Street. ⊠ *523 Truman Ave., Old Town* ☎ *305/294–0399* ⊕ *www.amscooterskeywest.com* ⌨ *Bicycles from $15, scooters from $35, electric cars from $139.*

Eaton Bikes

BIKING | **FAMILY** | Tandem, three-wheel, and children's bikes are available in addition to the standard beach cruisers and hybrid bikes. Delivery is free for all Key West rentals. ⊠ *830 Eaton St., Old Town* ☎ *305/294–8188* ⊕ *www.eatonbikes.com* ⌨ *From $25 per day.*

Fishing

Key West Bait & Tackle

FISHING | Prepare to catch a big one with this outfitter's live bait, frozen bait, and fishing equipment. Rod and reel rentals start at

$15 for a day ($5 each additional day). Stop by the on-site Live Bait Lounge, where you can sip a $3.25 ice-cold beer while telling fish tales. ⊠ *241 Margaret St., Historic Seaport* ☎ *305/292–1961* ⊕ *www.keywestbaitandtackle.com.*

★ Key West Pro Guides

FISHING | FAMILY | This outfitter offers four-, five-, six-, or eight-hour private charters, and you can choose from more than a dozen captains. Trips include flats, backcountry, reef, offshore fishing, and excursions to the Dry Tortugas. Whatever your fishing pleasure, the captains will hook you up. ⊠ *31 Miriam St., Stock Island* ☎ *866/259–4205* ⊕ *www.keywestproguides.com* 🖭 *From $500.*

Golf

Key West Golf Club

GOLF | Key West isn't a major golf destination, but there is one course on Stock Island designed by Rees Jones that will downright surprise you with its water challenges and tropical beauty. It's also the only "Caribbean" golf course in the United States, boasting 200 acres of unique Florida foliage and wildlife. Hole 8 is the famous "Mangrove Hole," which will give you stories to tell. It's a 143-yard par 3 that is played completely over a mass of mangroves with their gnarly, intertwined roots and branches. Bring extra balls and book your tee time early in peak season. Nike rental clubs are available. ⊠ *6450 E. College Rd., Stock Island* ☎ *305/294–5232* ⊕ *www.keywestgolf.com* 🖭 *$75* ⅄ *18 holes, 6500 yards, par 70.*

Kayaking

Key West Eco Tours

KAYAKING | FAMILY | The sail-kayak-snorkel excursions offered by this company take you into backcountry flats and mangrove forests without the crowds. The 4½-hour trips include a light lunch, equipment, and even dry camera bags. Private sunset sails, backcountry boating adventures, kayak, and paddleboard tours are available, too. ⊠ *231 Margaret St., Historic Seaport* ☎ *305/294–7245* ⊕ *www.keywestecotours.com* 🖭 *From $65.*

Lazy Dog

KAYAKING | FAMILY | Take a two-hour backcountry mangrove ecotour or a four-hour guided sea kayak–snorkel tour around the mangrove islands just east of Key West. Costs include transportation, bottled water, a snack, and supplies, including snorkeling gear. Paddleboard tours, PaddleYoga, and PaddleFit classes are also available, as are maps and rentals for self-touring. ✉ *5114 Overseas Hwy., Stock Island* ☎ *305/295–9898* ⊕ *www.lazydog.com* 🖙 *From $50.*

Sailing

★ Bluesail Yachting

SAILING | FAMILY | Bluesail offers everything from multi-day boat charters to four-hour private sunset sails complete with chef-made appetizers, wine, and beer. Its vessels have multi-occupancy cabins, full bathrooms, air-conditioning, and fully enclosed living spaces. The company is also an accredited American Sailing Association sailing school. ✉ *7005 Shrimp Rd., Stock Island* ☎ *813/601–5243* ⊕ *www.bluesailcharter.com* 🖙 *$1,500.*

Classic Harbor Line

SAILING | The *Schooner America 2.0* is refined and elegant, with comfortable seating that makes it a favorite for sails between November and April. Its two-hour sunset cruises are especially popular—with both locals and visitors. Reserve well in advance. ✉ *202-R Williams St., Historic Seaport* ☎ *305/293–7245* ⊕ *www. sail-keywest.com* 🖙 *Day sails from $44, sunset sails from $76.*

Dancing Dolphin Spirit Charters

BOATING | FAMILY | Victoria Impallomeni-Spencer, a wilderness guide and environmental marine science walking encyclopedia, invites up to six nature lovers aboard the *Imp II,* a 25-foot Aquasport, for four- and seven-hour ecotours that frequently include encounters with wild dolphins. ✉ *Hurricane Hole Marina, MM 4 OS, 5130 Overseas Hwy., Stock Island* ☎ *305/304–7562, 305/745–9901* ⊕ *www.dancingdolphinspirits.com* 🖙 *From $600.*

★ Sebago Watersports

SAILING | FAMILY | A one-stop-shop for all your sailing and snorkeling adventure needs, this popular company offers catamaran and schooner excursions, Key West sunset sails, snorkel trips to the living reef, parasailing, and more. Sebago's ships are spacious and state-of-the-art, with an experienced, friendly crew. ✉ *205 Elizabeth St., Historic Seaport* ☎ *305/294–5687* ⊕ *keywestsebago. com* 🖙 *From $50.*

Wind & Wine Sunset Sail

SAILING | Set sail on a historic 65-foot schooner and catch Key West's famous sunset as you drink wines from around the world (eight are presented during each sailing, three whites, four reds, and a champagne). Nosh on nibbles like Gouda and crackers, Brie and apples, and sausage rounds. Beer is also available.

✉ *Margaritaville Marina, 245 Front St., Old Town* ☎ *305/304–7999* ⊕ *www.dangercharters.com* 🎫 *$85.*

Scuba Diving and Snorkeling

Captain's Corner

DIVING & SNORKELING | FAMILY | This PADI-certified dive shop has classes in several languages and twice-daily snorkel and dive trips to reefs and wrecks aboard a 60-foot dive boat, the *Sea Eagle.* Weights, belts, masks, and fins are included in the rates. ✉ *126 Ann St., Old Town* ☎ *305/296–8865* ⊕ *www.captainscorner.com* 🎫 *From $45.*

Dive Key West

DIVING & SNORKELING | FAMILY | In business for more than 40 years and dedicated to coral reef preservation, this full-service dive center offers snorkel excursions and scuba trips, instruction, gear rental, sales, and repair. ✉ *3128 N. Roosevelt Blvd., New Town* ☎ *305/296–3823* ⊕ *www.divekeywest.com* 🎫 *Snorkeling from $69, scuba from $249.*

★ Honest Eco Tours

SNORKELING | FAMILY | Honest Eco's four-hour Dolphin Watch & Snorkel Tours take place aboard , a lithium-ion-battery-powered hybrid charter boat. You can watch wild dolphins as they play, sleep, hunt, and mate in Key West's tranquil, turquoise waters, and spend some time snorkeling in a tranquil spot. ✉ *231 Margaret St., Historic Seaport* ☎ *305/294–6306* ⊕ *honesteco.org* 🎫 *$99.*

Snuba of Key West

SCUBA DIVING | FAMILY | If you've always wanted to dive but never found the time to get certified, Snuba is for you. You can dive safely using a regulator tethered to a floating air tank with a simple orientation. ✉ *Garrison Bight Marina, Palm Ave. between Eaton St. and N. Roosevelt Blvd., New Town* ☎ *305/292–4616* ⊕ *www.snubakeywest.com* 🎫 *From $109.*

Dry Tortugas National Park

70 miles southwest of Key West.

The Dry Tortugas lie in the central time zone. Key West Seaplane pilots like to tell their passengers that they land 15 minutes before they take off. If you can't do the time-consuming and (by air, at least, expensive) trip, the national park operates an interpretive center in the Historic Seaport at Old Key West Bight.

GETTING HERE AND AROUND

The *Yankee Freedom III* ferryboat departs from a marina in Old Town and does day-trips to Garden Key. Key West Seaplane Adventures has half- and full-day trips to the Dry Tortugas, departing from the Key West airport.

CONTACTS Key West Seaplane Adventures. ⊠ *3471 S. Roosevelt Blvd., New Town* ☎ *305/615–7429* ⊕ *keywestseaplanecharters. com.* **Yankee Freedom III.** ⊠ *Ticket booth, 240 Margaret St., Historic Seaport* ☎ *305/294–7009, 800/634–0939* ⊕ *www.drytortugas. com.*

Sights

★ Dry Tortugas National Park

NATIONAL PARK | FAMILY | This park, 70 miles off the shores of Key West, consists of seven small islands. Most people spend their time on Garden Key, touring the 19th-century Fort Jefferson, the largest brick building in the Western Hemisphere, then heading out to snorkel on the protected reef. The brick fort acts like a gigantic, almost 16-acre reef. Around its moat walls, coral grows and schools of snapper, grouper, and wrasse hang out.

Serious snorkelers and divers head out farther offshore to epic formations, including Palmata Patch, one of the few surviving concentrations of elkhorn coral in the Keys. Day-trippers congregate on the sandy beach to relax in the sun and enjoy picnics. Overnight tent campers have use of restroom facilities and achieve a total getaway from noise, lights, and civilization in general.

The park has signposted a self-guided tour that takes about 45 minutes. You should budget more time if you're into photography because the scenic shots are hard to pass up. Ranger-guided tours are also available at certain times. Check in at the visitor center for a schedule. ⊠ *Key West* ☎ *305/242–7700* ⊕ *www.nps. gov/drto* 🎟 *$15.*

GATEWAYS TO THE KEYS

Updated by
Sara Liss

⊙ **Sights** 🍴 **Restaurants** 🛏 **Hotels** 🛍 **Shopping** 🍸 **Nightlife**
★★★★☆ ★★★★☆ ★★★★☆ ★★★★☆ ★★★★☆

WELCOME TO GATEWAYS TO THE KEYS

TOP REASONS TO GO

★ **Miami beaches:** Miami is famous for its fabulous stretches of beach, often lined with upscale resorts, especially along Collins Avenue. South Beach is perhaps the best-known strand and attracts both locals and tourists who spend the day sunning and swimming.

★ **Shopping on Lincoln Road:** Not only is this open-air pedestrian mall a great spot to shop for the latest fashions, but it's also brimming with chic restaurants, bars, and cafes, many of which have outdoor dining and drinking spaces for prime people-watching.

★ **Visiting Fruit and Spice Park:** This 37-acre park in Homestead's Redland historical agricultural district has more than 500 varieties of fruits, nuts, and spices. Take a tram tour to get the lay of the land, and sample some fresh fruit in the gift shop.

★ **Stocking up on tropical fruit:** Before heading down to the Keys, be sure to stop in to Robert Is Here Fruit Stand and Farm in Homestead. This local favorite has rare fruits like carambola and sapodilla, fresh smoothies, and an on-site petting zoo.

1 Miami. Mainland Miami is South Florida's commercial hub, while its sultry sister Miami Beach is famous for its beaches, dining, and nightlife. Miami Beach, and especially South Beach with its pastel-hued art deco buildings, is what most people think of when they think of Miami.

2 Homestead. Homestead lies at the crossroads between Miami and the Keys as well as Everglades and Biscayne National Parks. It has become a destination for tropical agro-tourism, with miles of fields growing fresh fruit and vegetables.

3 Florida City. Florida's Turnpike ends in Florida City, the southernmost town on the Miami–Dade County mainland, making it a hub for those visiting the Everglades, Biscayne National Park, and the Florida Keys. It's also home to Homestead–Miami Speedway, which hosts NASCAR races.

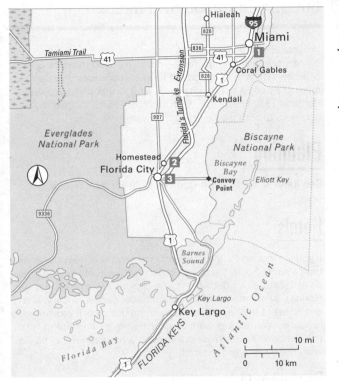

Many visitors flying into Florida to visit the Keys will likely pass through the buzzing metropolis of Miami.

In some cases, people choose to stay a while to absorb the culinary scene and hot nightlife—not to mention the expansive beaches, which the Keys do not have in abundance. Travelers on more of a budget may want to look a bit farther afield to either Homestead or Florida City, both south of Miami, the two major gateways to both the Keys and the Everglades.

Planning

See Travel Smart for information on flights and car rentals in Miami.

Hotels

If you are looking for the hot spots, then you need look no farther than Miami's South Beach, which is filled with both new high-rises and restored art deco gems. The choices in Homestead and Florida City are more pedestrian but also friendlier to the wallet and closer to the Keys. Given the driving distance, if you arrive late in Miami, you may just want to sleep before getting an early start to drive down to the Keys; in that case, a basic room may be just what the travel agent ordered.

Restaurants

Miami has a vibrant dining scene, with prices to match, but you can still find reasonably priced local restaurants and chains, mostly outside the trendy South Beach area. Most restaurants south of Miami are small, mom-and-pop establishments serving homey food or local specialties such as alligator, fish, stone crab, frogs' legs, and fresh Florida lobster from the Keys. There are plenty of chain restaurants and fast-food establishments, especially in the Homestead and Florida City areas.

Hotel and restaurant reviews have been shortened. For full information, visit Fodors.com. Hotel prices are the lowest cost of a standard double room in high season. Restaurant prices are the average cost of a main course at dinner or, if dinner is not served, at lunch.

What It Costs			
$	$$	$$$	$$$$
RESTAURANTS			
under $20	$20–$25	$26–$35	over $35
HOTELS			
under $200	$200–$300	$301–$400	over $400

Miami

In the 1950s, Miami was best known for alligator wrestlers and "U-pick" strawberry fields and citrus groves. Well, things have changed. Mainland Miami is now South Florida's commercial hub, while its sultry sister, Miami Beach, encompasses 17 islands in Biscayne Bay. Seducing winter refugees with its sunshine, beaches, palms, and nightlife, Miami Beach is what most people envision when they think of Miami.

◉ Sights

Art Deco Welcome Center and Museum

HISTORY MUSEUM | Run by the Miami Design Preservation League, the center provides information about the buildings in the district. There's also an official Art Deco Museum within the center, as well as a gift shop that sells art deco memorabilia and posters from the 1930s through '50s, as well as books on Miami's history. Several tours also start here, including a self-guided audio tour and regular morning walking tours at 10:30 daily (excluding Tuesday and Wednesday). ⌂ 1001 Ocean Dr., South Beach ☎ 305/672–2014, 305/531–3484 for tours ⊕ www.mdpl.org ⌂ Tours from $35.

Cuban Memorial Boulevard

MONUMENT | Four blocks in the heart of Little Havana are filled with monuments to Cuba's freedom fighters. South of Calle Ocho (8th Street), Southwest 13th Avenue becomes a ceiba tree–lined parkway known as Cuban Memorial Boulevard, divided at the center by a narrow grassy mall with a walking path through the various memorials. Among them is the Eternal Torch of the Brigade 2506, blazing with an endless flame and commemorating those who were killed in the failed Bay of Pigs invasion of 1961. Another is a bas-relief map of Cuba depicting each of its municipios. There's also a bronze statue in honor of Nestor (Tony) Izquierdo, who participated in the Bay of Pigs invasion and served in Nicaragua's

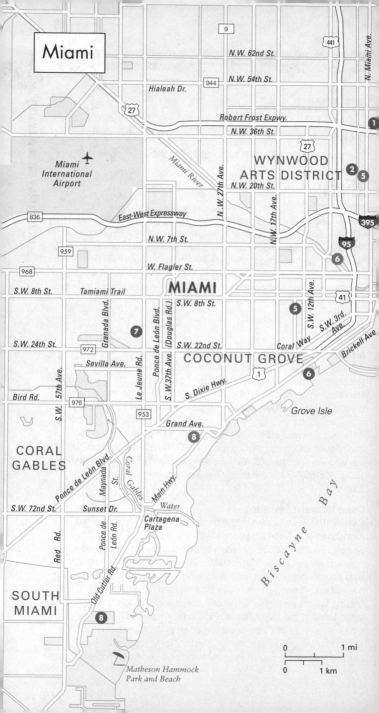

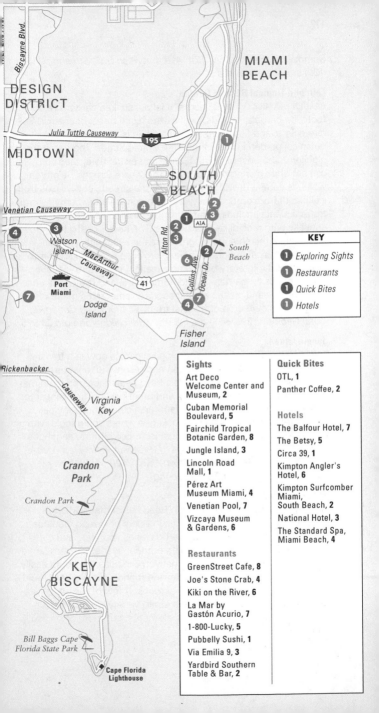

MIAMI
BEACH

DESIGN
DISTRICT

MIDTOWN

Biscayne Blvd.

Julia Tuttle Causeway 195

SOUTH
BEACH

Venetian Causeway

Watson
Island

MacArthur
Causeway

Port
Miami

Dodge
Island

Alton Rd.

A1A

Collins Ave.

Ocean Dr.

South
Beach

41

Fisher
Island

Rickenbacker

Causeway

Virginia
Key

Crandon
Park

Crandon Park

KEY
BISCAYNE

Bill Baggs Cape
Florida State Park

Cape Florida
Lighthouse

KEY

- 1 *Exploring Sights*
- 1 *Restaurants*
- 1 *Quick Bites*
- 1 *Hotels*

Sights

Art Deco
Welcome Center and
Museum, **2**

Cuban Memorial
Boulevard, **5**

Fairchild Tropical
Botanic Garden, **8**

Jungle Island, **3**

Lincoln Road
Mall, **1**

Pérez Art
Museum Miami, **4**

Venetian Pool, **7**

Vizcaya Museum
& Gardens, **6**

Restaurants

GreenStreet Cafe, **8**

Joe's Stone Crab, **4**

Kiki on the River, **6**

La Mar by
Gastón Acurio, **7**

1-800-Lucky, **5**

Pubbelly Sushi, **1**

Via Emilia 9, **3**

Yardbird Southern
Table & Bar, **2**

Quick Bites

OTL, **1**

Panther Coffee, **2**

Hotels

The Balfour Hotel, **7**

The Betsy, **5**

Circa 39, **1**

Kimpton Angler's
Hotel, **6**

Kimpton Surfcomber
Miami,
South Beach, **2**

National Hotel, **3**

The Standard Spa,
Miami Beach, **4**

Somozan forces. ⊠ *S.W. 13th Ave. between S.W. 8th and S.W. 12th sts., Little Havana.*

Fairchild Tropical Botanic Garden

GARDEN | FAMILY | With 83 acres of lakes, sunken gardens, a 560-foot vine pergola, orchids, bellflowers, coral trees, bougainvillea, rare palms, and flowering trees, Fairchild is the largest tropical botanical garden in the continental United States. The tram tour highlights the best of South Florida and exotic flora; then you can set off exploring on your own. The 2-acre Simons Rainforest, which is complete with a waterfall and a stream, showcases tropical plants from around the world. The conservatory contains rare tropical plants, including the Burmese *Amherstia nobilis,* flowering annually with orchidlike pink flowers. The Keys Coastal Habitat, created in a marsh and mangrove area in 1995 with assistance from the Tropical Audubon Society, provides food and shelter to resident and migratory birds. The excellent bookstore–gift shop carries books on gardening and horticulture, and The Glasshouse Café serves sandwiches and, seasonally, smoothies made from the garden's own crop of tropical fruits. ⊠ *10901 Old Cutler Rd., Coral Gables* ☎ *305/667–1651* ⊕ *www.fairchildgarden.org* ⊠ *$25.*

Jungle Island

ZOO | FAMILY | This interactive zoological park is now in a transitional phase as it develops into an eco resort with a waterfront hotel. Most of the large mammals have been relocated to animal sanctuaries, but the exotic birds and other wildlife, like kangaroos and tortoises, remain. In the meantime, you can book animal encounters and enhanced VIP packages where you mingle with an array of furry and feathered friends, including lemurs, flamingos, and sloths. ⊠ *Watson Island, 1111 Parrot Jungle Trail, off MacArthur Causeway (I–395), Downtown* ☎ *305/400–7000* ⊕ *www.jungleisland.com* ⊠ *$65, $10 parking.*

★ Lincoln Road Mall

PEDESTRIAN MALL | FAMILY | Lincoln Road has some of Miami's best people-watching. The eclectic interiors of myriad fabulous restaurants, colorful boutiques, art galleries, lounges, and cafés are often upstaged by the bustling outdoor scene. It's here, amid many alfresco dining enclaves, that you can pass the hours easily. Indeed, Lincoln Road is fun, lively, and friendly for everyone—old, young, gay, and straight—and their dogs. A few of the shops are owner-operated boutiques with a smart variety of clothing, furnishings, jewelry, and decorative elements, but more often you'll find typical chain stores.

Two landmarks worth checking out at the eastern end of Lincoln Road are the massive 1940s keystone building at No. 420, which has a 1945 Leo Birchansky mural in the lobby, and the 1921 mission-style Miami Beach Community Church at Drexel Avenue. The Lincoln Theatre (541–545 Lincoln Road, at Pennsylvania Avenue) is a classical four-story art deco gem with friezes that now houses an H&M. ⌧ *Lincoln Rd. between Washington Ave. and Alton Rd., South Beach* ⊕ *www.lincolnroadmall.com.*

★ Pérez Art Museum Miami (*PAMM*)

ART MUSEUM | FAMILY | This uber-high-design architectural masterpiece on Biscayne Bay is a sight to behold. Double-story, cylindrical hanging gardens sway from high atop the museum, anchored to stylish wooden trusses that help create this gotta-see-it-to-believe-it indoor-outdoor museum. Large sculptures, Asian-inspired gardens, sexy white benches, and steel frames surround the property. Inside, the 120,000-square-foot space houses multicultural art from the 20th and 21st centuries. Most of the interior space is devoted to temporary exhibitions, which have included the likes of *Ai Weiwei: According to What?* and *Grids: A Selection of Paintings by Lynne Golob Gelfman.* Even if you aren't a "museum type," come check out this magnum opus over lunch at Verde, the museum's sensational waterfront restaurant and bar. ⌧ *1103 Biscayne Blvd., Downtown* ☎ *305/375–3000* ⊕ *www. pamm.org* ⌧ *$16* ⊙ *Closed Tues. and Wed.*

Venetian Pool

POOL | FAMILY | Sculpted from a rock quarry in 1923 and fed by artesian wells, this 820,000-gallon municipal pool remains quite popular because of its themed architecture—a fantasy version of a waterfront Italian village—created by Denman Fink. The pool has earned a place on the National Register of Historic Places and showcases a nice collection of vintage photos depicting 1920s beauty pageants and swank soirées held long ago. Paul Whiteman played here. Johnny Weissmuller and Esther Williams swam here, and you should, too (note: children must be at least 3 years old and 38 inches tall). A snack bar, lockers, and showers make these historic splash grounds user friendly as well, and there's free parking across De Soto Boulevard. Call before visiting to confirm that renovations (which closed the pool in late 2022 through early 2023) are complete. ⌧ *2701 De Soto Blvd., at Toledo St., Coral Gables* ☎ *305/460–5306* ⊕ *www.coralgables.com/venetian-pool* ⌧ *$21.*

Vizcaya Museum and Gardens features more than 10 acres of formal gardens overlooking Biscayne Bay.

★ Vizcaya Museum & Gardens

HISTORIC HOME | FAMILY | Of the 10,000 people living in Miami between 1912 and 1916, about 1,000 of them were gainfully employed by Chicago industrialist James Deering to build this European-inspired residence that resembles a tropical version of Versailles. Once comprising 180 acres, this National Historic Landmark now occupies a 30-acre tract that includes a rock-land hammock (native forest) and more than 10 acres of formal gardens with fountains overlooking Biscayne Bay. The house, open to the public, contains 70 rooms, 34 of which are filled with paintings, sculpture, antique furniture, and other fine and decorative arts. The collection spans 2,000 years and represents the Renaissance, baroque, rococo, and neoclassical periods. The 90-minute self-guided Discover Vizcaya Audio Tour is available in multiple languages for an additional $5. Moonlight tours, offered on evenings that are nearest the full moon, provide a magical look at the gardens; call for reservations. ⊠ *3251 S. Miami Ave., Coconut Grove* ☎ *305/250–9133* ⊕ *www.vizcaya.org* ⌷ *$25* ⊗ *Closed Tues.*

Beaches

Almost every east–west side street in Miami Beach dead-ends at the ocean. Sandy shores also stretch along the southern side of the Rickenbacker Causeway to Key Biscayne, where you'll find more popular beaches. Greater Miami is best known for its ocean beaches, but there's freshwater swimming here, too, in pools and lakes. Below are the highlights for the get-wet set.

★ Bill Baggs Cape Florida State Park

BEACH | FAMILY | Thanks to inviting beaches, sunsets, and a tranquil lighthouse, this park at Key Biscayne's southern tip is worth the drive. In fact, the 1-mile stretch of pure beachfront has been named several times in Dr. Beach's revered America's Top 10 Beaches list. It has 18 picnic pavilions available as daily rentals, two cafés that serve light lunches (including several Cuban specialties), and plenty of space to plant the umbrellas and chairs that you can rent. The walking and bicycle paths provide wonderful views of Miami's dramatic skyline. From the southern end of the park you can see a handful of houses rising over the bay on wooden stilts, the remnants of Stiltsville, built in the 1940s and now protected by the Stiltsville Trust. The nonprofit group was established in 2003 to preserve the structures, which showcase the park's rich history. Bill Baggs also has bicycle rentals, a playground, fishing piers, and guided tours of the Cape Florida Lighthouse, South Florida's oldest structure. The lighthouse was erected in 1845 to replace an earlier one damaged in an 1836 battle with the Seminole tribe. Free tours are offered at the restored cottage and lighthouse Thursday to Monday at 10 am and 1 pm. Be there a half hour beforehand. **Amenities:** food and drink; lifeguards; parking (no fee); showers; toilets. **Best for:** solitude; sunset; walking. ⊠ 1200 S. Crandon Blvd., Key Biscayne ☎ 305/361–5811 ⊕ www.floridastateparks.org/park/Cape-Florida ⊴ $8 per vehicle, $2 per pedestrian.

Matheson Hammock Park

BEACH | FAMILY | Kids love the gentle waves and warm (albeit often murky) waters of this beach in Coral Gables suburbia, near the Fairchild Tropical Botanic Garden. But the beach is only part of the draw—the park includes a boardwalk trail, a playground, and a golf course. Plus, the park is a prime spot for kiteboarding. The man-made lagoon, or "atoll pool," is perfect for inexperienced swimmers, and it's one of the best places in mainland Miami for a picnic. Most tourists don't make the trek here; this park caters more to locals who don't want to travel all the way to Miami Beach. The park also offers a full-service marina. ■TIP→ **With an emphasis on family fun, it's not the best place for singles. Amenities:** parking (fee); toilets. **Best for:** swimming. ⊠ 9610 Old Cutler Rd., Coral Gables ☎ 305/665–5475 ⊕ www.miamidade.gov/parks/matheson-hammock.asp ⊴ $5 per vehicle weekdays, $7 weekends.

★ South Beach

BEACH | Hugging the turquoise waters along Ocean Drive from 5th to 15th Streets, this is one of the most popular beaches in America, known for its colorful lifeguard towers and social sunbathers. With the influx of luxe hotels and hot spots from 1st to 5th and 16th to 25th Streets, the stand-and-pose scene is now bigger than ever, stretching yet another dozen-plus blocks. The white sandy stretch fills up quickly on the weekends with a blend of European tourists, young hipsters, and sun-drenched locals. Separating the shore from the traffic of Ocean Drive is palm-fringed Lummus Park, with its volleyball nets and winding bike path. There are access points every few streets, including 14th Street, 12th Street, and so on. Locals hang out on the 3rd Street beach, in an area called SoFi (South of Fifth). Dogs are not allowed on the beach. **Amenities:** food and drink; lifeguards; parking (fee); showers; toilets. **Best for:** partiers; sunrise; swimming; walking. ⊠ *Ocean Dr. from 5th to 15th Sts., then Collins Ave. to 25th St., South Beach* 🌊 *Free.*

Restaurants

GreenStreet Cafe

$ | **MEDITERRANEAN** | A tried-and-true locals' hangout since it was founded in the early 1990s—with regulars including athletes, politicians, entrepreneurs, artists, and other prominent area names—this cozy café serves simple French-Mediterranean delights. Despite the restaurant's see-and-be-seen reputation, diners are encouraged to sit back and simply enjoy the experience with relaxed decor, good food, and friendly service. **Known for:** fruity cocktails; Nutella French toast; late-night lounging and noshing. ⑤ *Average main: $19* ⊠ *3468 Main Hwy., Coconut Grove* ☎ *305/444–0244* ⊕ *www.greenstreetcafe.net.*

★ Joe's Stone Crab

$$$$ | **SEAFOOD** | In South Beach's decidedly new-money scene, the stately Joe's Stone Crab is an old-school testament to good food and good service. Stone crabs, served with legendary mustard sauce, crispy hash browns, and creamed spinach, remain the staple at South Beach's most storied restaurant (which dates from 1913). **Known for:** best-of-the-best stone crab claws; key lime pie; no reservations (arrive very early). ⑤ *Average main: $46* ⊠ *11 Washington Ave., South Beach* ☎ *305/673–0365, 305/673–4611 for takeout* ⊕ *www.joesstonecrab.com* 🕓 *Closed mid-May–mid-Oct. No lunch Sun. and Mon.*

★ Kiki on the River

$$$ | GREEK | This posh taverna featuring grilled fish and classic mezes is also a good place for celebrity sightings—from local basketball stars to pop music moguls. The lush waterfront hideaway has an inviting patio with blooming bougainvillea, whitewashed walls, secluded "cabana" tables, and navy-cushioned seating. **Known for:** grilled branzino; Sunday evening parties; river views. $ *Average main: $26* ⊠ *450 N.W. North River Dr., Downtown* ☎ *305/502–3243* ⊕ *kikiontheriver.com.*

La Mar by Gastón Acurio

$$$ | PERUVIAN | Peruvian chef Gastón Acurio's downtown Miami outpost occupies a gleaming waterfront spot at Brickell Key's Mandarin Oriental. The main dining room is awash in shades of watery greens, sandy grays, and beiges, and wood, but it's the enticing outdoor terrace that offers views of downtown and is the perfect backdrop to chef Diego Oka's contemporary Peruvian dishes with colorful tweaks. **Known for:** creative ceviche; waterfront views; posh service. $ *Average main: $28* ⊠ *Mandarin Oriental, 500 Brickell Key Dr., Brickell Key* ☎ *305/913–8358* ⊕ *www.mandarinoriental.com.*

1-800-Lucky

$ | ASIAN FUSION | This trendy, 10,000-square-foot food hall has indoor and outdoor seating and a booming hip-hop soundtrack. Seven vendors hawking pan-Asian dishes—from ramen to poke bowls to Filipino burgers—two full bars, and a karaoke lounge surround the open dining room, and the patio provides a view of the Japanese soft-serve stall serving matcha green tea ice cream in fish-shape waffle cones. **Known for:** lively atmosphere; Asian dishes; live DJ music. $ *Average main: $17* ⊠ *143 NW 23rd St., Wynwood* ⊕ *www.1800lucky.com* 🏛 *casual.*

★ Pubbelly Sushi

$$ | ASIAN FUSION | On a residential street in SoBe's western reaches, this petite eatery attracts the who's who of beach socialites, hipsters, and the occasional tourist coming to chow down on inventive Asian-Latin small plates, sushi rolls, and grilled skewers of meat and seafood by executive chef-owner José Mendin. From bigeye tuna spicy rolls to short-rib and truffle dumplings, the menu constantly pushes the envelope on inventive cuisine, and locals simply can't get enough. **Known for:** long waits; pork belly bao buns; butter "krab" roll. $ *Average main: $21* ⊠ *1424 20th St., South Beach* ☎ *305/531–9282* ⊕ *pubbellyglobal.com.*

Via Emilia 9

$$ | ITALIAN | FAMILY | If you're longing for a *true* taste of Italy's Emilia Romagna region and a respite from the overpriced SoBe dining scene, head to this adorable hole-in-the-wall restaurant off Alton Road. The pastas and sauces are made fresh daily, using only the best ingredients imported from the chef's homeland supplemented with local produce. **Known for:** ravioli of the day; homemade flatbreads; variety of stuffed pastas. $ *Average main: $22* ⊠ *1120 15th St., South Beach* ☎ *786/216–7150* ⊕ *www.viaemilia9.com.*

Yardbird Southern Table & Bar

$$$ | AMERICAN | There's a helluva lot of southern lovin' from the low country at this funky South Beach spot, where Miami's A-list puts calorie-counting aside to indulge in comfort foods and innovative drinks. The family-style menu is divided between small plates, "the bird" plates, and sides and snacks, but have no doubt that "the bird" takes center stage (or plate) here—you'll rave about Llewellyn's fine fried chicken, which requires a 27-hour marination and slow-cooking process, for weeks to come. **Known for:** smoked brisket biscuits; bourbon cocktails; chicken 'n' watermelon 'n' waffles. $ *Average main: $27* ⊠ *1600 Lenox Ave., South Beach* ☎ *305/538–5220* ⊕ *www.runchickenrun.com.*

☕ Coffee and Quick Bites

OTL

$ | AMERICAN | The name stands for "out to lunch," and, indeed, you could hang for quite the lunch break at this Design District haunt that serves coffee drinks, pastries, and sandwiches in an Instagram-worthy atmosphere. Don't miss the toast topped with superseed butter, a gluttonous, if healthy, alternative to your usual PB&J standby. **Known for:** avocado toast; strong coffee; people-watching. $ *Average main: $12* ⊠ *160 N.E. 40th St., Design District* ☎ *305/953–7620* ⊕ *www.otlmia.com* ☾ *No dinner.*

Panther Coffee

$ | AMERICAN | The java spot that launched Miami's caffeine revolution, this no-frills Wynwood flagship is a good pit stop for iced cold brew as you're perusing art and graffiti murals in the district. The shop also serves cakes, cookies, wine, and beer, all in a friendly atmosphere with free Wi-Fi and local art on the walls. **Known for:** great baristas; ethically sourced coffee; colorful crowd. $ *Average main: $6* ⊠ *2390 N.W. 2nd Ave., Wynwood* ☎ *305/677–3952* ⊕ *www.panthercoffee.com.*

Hotels

The Balfour Hotel
$ | HOTEL | In South Beach's SoFi (South of Fifth) neighborhood, the boutique Lord Balfour hotel is a great fit for young travelers who want to get out and experience South Beach (as opposed to sitting at a resort all day) and then return to stylish digs. **Pros:** great European crowd; pleasant interior design; affordable pricing. **Cons:** small rooms and smaller bathrooms; occasional street noise from some rooms; small pool. ⑤ *Rooms from: $175* ✉ *350 Ocean Dr., South Beach* ☎ *855/471–2739* ⊕ *www.thebalfourmiamibeach. com* ⇨ *64 rooms* ⑩ *No Meals.*

★ The Betsy
$$ | HOTEL | The city's artiest boutique hotel is also, arguably, Ocean Drive's classiest property, with a modern new wing, a rooftop pool, and an Italian trattoria. **Pros:** arts programming; excellent in-house dining; attentive staff. **Cons:** not directly on beach; rooms can be small; pricey. ⑤ *Rooms from: $300* ✉ *1440 Ocean Dr., South Beach* ☎ *305/531–6100* ⊕ *thebetsyhotel.com* ⇨ *130 rooms* ⑩ *No Meals.*

Circa 39
$$ | HOTEL | Located in the heart of Mid-Beach, this stylish yet affordable boutique hotel has tropical-inspired rooms, as well as a pool and sun deck complete with cabanas and umbrella-shaded chaises that invite all-day lounging. **Pros:** lounge areas in the WunderGarden; beach chairs provided; art deco fireplace. **Cons:** not on the beach side of Collins Avenue; bathrooms have showers only; no spa. ⑤ *Rooms from: $299* ✉ *3900 Collins Ave., Mid-Beach* ☎ *305/538–4900* ⊕ *www.circa39.com* ⇨ *97 rooms* ⑩ *No Meals.*

★ Kimpton Angler's Hotel
$$$$ | HOTEL | At this enclave of old and new South Beach, a contemporary, 85-room tower with a rooftop pool neighbors several 1930s-era villas and modern low-rise units, together capturing the feel of a sophisticated private villa community. **Pros:** gardened private retreat; pet-friendly (no fee); daily complimentary wine hour. **Cons:** no gym; not directly on beach; most units have only showers. ⑤ *Rooms from: $427* ✉ *660 Washington Ave., South Beach* ☎ *305/534–9600* ⊕ *www.anglershotelmiami.com* ⇨ *132 rooms* ⑩ *No Meals.*

Kimpton Surfcomber Miami, South Beach
$$ | HOTEL | As part of the hip Kimpton Hotel group, South Beach's legendary Surfcomber hotel reflects a vintage luxe aesthetic and an ocean-side freshness as well as a reasonable price point that

packs the place with a young, sophisticated, yet unpretentious crowd. **Pros:** frozen spiked cappuccino at High Tide Bar; no pet fee; daily complimentary activities offered. **Cons:** small bathrooms; front desk often busy; often congested valet. ⑤ *Rooms from: $299 ✉ 1717 Collins Ave., South Beach ☎ 305/532–7715 ⊕ www.surfcomber.com ⤳ 186 rooms* ⑩ *No Meals.*

National Hotel

$$$ | HOTEL | The adults-only National Hotel is a glorious time capsule that honors its distinct art deco heritage (the building itself and wood pieces in the lobby date from 1939, and new chocolate- and gold-hue furnishings look period-appropriate) while trying to keep up with SoBe's glossy newcomers (rotating art installations complement the throwback glamour). **Pros:** cabana suites; beautiful night-lights around pool area; art deco Blues Bar. **Cons:** street noise on the weekends; gym located downstairs in back of house; no spa. ⑤ *Rooms from: $355 ✉ 1677 Collins Ave., South Beach ☎ 305/532–2311 ⊕ www.nationalhotel.com ⤳ 152 rooms* ⑩ *No Meals.*

The Standard Spa, Miami Beach

$$$ | RESORT | An extension of André Balazs's trendy and hip—yet budget-conscious—brand, this shabby-chic boutique hotel is a mile from South Beach on an island just over the Venetian Causeway and has among South Florida's most renowned spas, trendiest bars, and hottest pool scenes. **Pros:** free bike rentals; swank pool scene; great spa. **Cons:** slight trek to South Beach; small rooms with no views; nonguests visiting property spa and restaurants. ⑤ *Rooms from: $324 ✉ 40 Island Ave., Belle Isle ☎ 305/673–1717 ⊕ www.standardhotels.com/miami/properties/miami-beach ⤳ 105 rooms* ⑩ *No Meals.*

Nightlife

One of Greater Miami's most popular pursuits is barhopping. Options range from intimate enclaves to showy see-and-be-seen lounges and loud, raucous frat parties. Undoubtedly, Miami's pulse pounds with nonstop nightlife that reflects the area's potent cultural mix. On sultry, humid nights who can resist Cuban salsa with some disco and hip-hop thrown in for good measure? It's no wonder many clubs are still rocking at 5 am. If you're looking for a relatively calm evening, your best bet is one of the chic hotel bars on Collins Avenue.

Shopping

Miami has evolved into a world-class shopping destination. Give your plastic a workout at the many high-profile tenants on the densely packed stretch of **Collins Avenue** between 5th and 10th Streets or along the eight-block-long pedestrianized **Lincoln Road Mall,** which is home to more than 200 shops, art galleries, restaurants and cafés, as well as the renovated Colony Theatre.

Homestead

30 miles southwest of Miami.

At a crossroads between Miami and the Keys, as well as Everglades and Biscayne National Parks, Homestead has become a destination for tropical agro- and ecotourism. The area also has shopping centers, residential developments, hotel chains, and the Homestead–Miami Speedway. When car races are scheduled, hotels hike rates and require minimum stays.

◉ Sights

★ Dante Fascell Visitor Center

VISITOR CENTER | **FAMILY** | From the wide veranda of Biscayne National Park's mainland visitor center, you can soak up views of the mangroves and the bay before signing up for tours, snorkeling excursions, and ranger programs. The compact but very informative collection in the small museum offers insights into the park's natural, geological, and human history. Restrooms with showers, a gift shop, picnic tables, grills, and children's activities are also found here. ⊠ *Convoy Point, 9700 S.W. 328th St., Sir Lancelot Jones Way, Homestead* ☎ *305/230–1144* ⊕ *www.nps.gov/bisc* ⊠ *Free.*

Schnebly Redland's Winery & Brewery

WINERY | Homestead's tropical bounty is transformed into wine at this flourishing enterprise that started producing wines with lychee, mango, guava, and other local fruits as a way to eliminate waste from family groves each year. Over the course of a few decades, the winery expanded to include a tasting room, a full-service restaurant, and a lush plaza picnic area landscaped in coral rock, tropical plants, and waterfalls. It's also home to popular beer brand Miami Brewing Company. ⊠ *30205 S.W. 217th Ave., Homestead* ☎ *305/242–1224* ⊕ *www.schneblywinery.com* ⊠ *Weekend tours $16 per person.*

 Restaurants

Shiver's BBQ

$ | **BARBECUE** | **FAMILY** | Piggin' out since the 1950s, Shiver's BBQ is celebrated near and far for its slowly smoked pork, beef, and chicken. Be forewarned as you settle in at the communal tables; this spot is no place to cut calories. **Known for:** hickory-smoked barbecue; baby back ribs; takeout service. ⑤ *Average main: $19* ✉ *28001 S. Dixie Hwy., Homestead* ☎ *305/248–2272* ⊕ *shiversbq.com.*

Hotels

The Hotel Redland

$ | **HOTEL** | Of downtown Homestead's smattering of mom-and-pop lodges, this historic inn is by far the most desirable. **Pros:** historic charm; conveniently located; excellent dining. **Cons:** traffic noise; small rooms; potentially haunted. ⑤ *Rooms from: $150* ✉ *5 S. Flagler Ave., Homestead* ☎ *305/246–1904* ⊕ *www.cityhallbistromartinibar.com* 🛏 *13 rooms* ¶◎¶ *No Meals.*

Shopping

Robert Is Here Fruit Stand and Farm

FOOD | **FAMILY** | This historic stand and farm sells more than 100 types of jams, jellies, honeys, and salad dressings along with farm-fresh veggies and dozens of tropical fruits. The list of rare finds includes carambola, lychee, eggfruit, sapodilla, and tamarind. Try them in a smoothie or milk shake. ✉ *19200 S.W. 344th St., Homestead* ☎ *305/246–1592* ⊕ *www.robertishere.com.*

Activities

AUTO RACING

Homestead–Miami Speedway

AUTO RACING | **FAMILY** | Buzzing more than 300 days a year, the 600-acre speedway has 65,000 grandstand seats, club seating, and two tracks—a 2.21-mile road course and a 1.5-mile oval. ✉ *1 Ralph Sanchez Speedway Blvd., Homestead* ☎ *305/230–5000, 866/409–7223 ticket office* ⊕ *www.homesteadmiamispeedway.com.*

BOATING

Homestead Bayfront Park

WATER SPORTS | **FAMILY** | Boaters, anglers, and beachgoers give high praise to this recreational area with a natural atoll pool and beach, a marina, the La Playa Grill Seafood & Bar restaurant, a playground, and a picnic pavilion with grills, showers, and restrooms. ⊠ *9698 S.W. 328th St., Homestead* ☎ *305/230–3033* ⊕ *www. miamidade.gov/parks/homestead-bayfront.asp* 🗪 *$7 per car on weekends; $5 per car on weekdays.*

Florida City

2 miles southwest of Homestead.

Florida's Turnpike ends in Florida City, the southernmost town on the Miami–Dade County mainland, spilling thousands of vehicles onto U.S. 1 and eventually west to Everglades National Park, east to Biscayne National Park, or south to the Florida Keys. Although Florida City begins immediately south of Homestead, the difference in towns couldn't be more noticeable. As the last outpost before 18 miles of mangroves and water, this stretch of U.S. 1 is lined with fast-food eateries, service stations, hotels, bars, dive shops, and restaurants.

◉ Sights

Tropical Everglades Visitor Center

VISITOR CENTER | Managed by the nonprofit Tropical Everglades Visitor Association, this pastel-pink information center with teal signage offers abundant printed material, plus tips from volunteer experts on exploring South Florida, especially Homestead, Florida City, and the Florida Keys. ⊠ *160 S.E. 1st Ave., Florida City* ☎ *305/245–9180* ⊕ *tropicaleverglades.com.*

Restaurants

Farmers' Market Restaurant

$ | **SEAFOOD** | This quaint eatery is inside the farmers' market on the edge of town, and it's big on serving fresh vegetables and seafood. A family of anglers runs the place, so fish and shellfish are only hours from the ocean. **Known for:** early hours for breakfast; seafood-centric menu; using fresh produce from the market. ⑤ *Average main: $13* ⊠ *300 N. Krome Ave., Ste. 17, Florida City* ☎ *305/242–0008* ⊕ *www.facebook.com/ floridacityfarmersmarketrestaurant.*

Hotels

Best Western Gateway to the Keys

$ | **HOTEL** | For easy access to Everglades and Biscayne National Parks, as well as the Keys, you'll be well situated at this relatively modern, two-story motel close to Florida's Turnpike. **Pros:** conveniently located; free Wi-Fi and breakfast; attractive poolscape. **Cons:** traffic noise; books up fast in high season; no pets. $ *Rooms from: $120* ⊠ *411 S. Krome Ave., Florida City* ☎ *305/246–5100* ⊕ *www.bestwestern.com* ⇔ *114 rooms* ¦O¦ *Free Breakfast.*

Quality Inn Florida City

$ | **HOTEL** | Nestled in a complex of hotels, gas stations, and eateries just off U.S. 1, this two-story Quality Inn has a friendly front-desk staff offering tips on Everglades and Keys adventures or race action at the nearby track. **Pros:** conveniently located; modern decor; affordable rates. **Cons:** no elevator; noisy location; no pets allowed. $ *Rooms from: $75* ⊠ *333 S.E. 1st Ave., Florida City* ☎ *786/465–7600* ⊕ *www.choicehotels.com* ⇔ *123 rooms* ¦O¦ *Free Breakfast.*

Index

Photo Credits

Front Cover: Marco Simoni / Huber / eStock Photo [**Description:** Fort Jefferson in Dry Tortugas National Park, Florida Keys, Florida, USA]. **Back cover, from left to right:** Chuck Wagner/ Shutterstock. Irina Wilhauk/Shutterstock. Pisaphotography/Shutterstock. **Spine:** PHB.cz (Richard Semik)/Shutterstock. **Interior, from left to right:** PBorowka/Shutterstock (1). Rob O'Neal/Florida Keys News Bureau (2-3). **Chapter 1: Experience the Florida Keys:** Meinzahn/iStockphoto (6-7). NicholasGeraldinePhotos/shutterstock (8-9). Michael Dwyer/Alamy (9). Todd Taulman Photogrpahy (9). Melissa Schalke/iStockphoto (10). George Burba/Shutterstock (10). Simon Dannhauer/Shutterstock (10). Irina Wilhauk/shutterstock (10). Stephen Frink/TDC/Visit Florida (11). The Floridian/ shutterstock (12). Vanilla Fire/Shutterstock (12). Robert Hoetink/Shutterstock (12). Michael Gordon/ shutterstock (12). EB Adventure Photography/Shutterstock (13). Phillip Sunkel IV/shutterstock (13). Comeirrez/Shutterstock (18). Brent Hofacker/Shutterstock (18). Mrs. Mac's Kitchens (18). Voloshin311/Shutterstock (18). Olyina/Shutterstock (19). Alena Haurylik/shutterstock (19). Bonchan/ Shutterstock (19). Hans Geel/Shutterstock (19). Simon Dannhauer/Shutterstock (20). Luke Popwell/ Dreamstime (20). Chuck Wagner/Shutterstock (20). Courtesy of Long Key State Park (20). Simon Dannhauer/Shutterstock (21). **Chapter 3: The Upper Keys:** Inspired By Maps/shutterstock (43). William Lermond/Florida State Parks (51). Lazyllama/Shutterstock (63). **Chapter 4: The Middle Keys:** SimonDannhauer/Dreamstime (77). Tbintb/Dreamstime (84). Seastock/iStockphoto (91). Andy Newman/Florida Keys News Bureau (94). **Chapter 5: The Lower Keys:** Marilyn Scavo/iStockphoto (97). Simon Dannhauer/Shutterstock (103). Mia2you/Shutterstock (106). **Chapter 6: Key West:** Pisaphotography/Shutterstock (113). Andylid/istockphoto (121). f11photo/Shutterstock (125). Robert Hoetink/Shutterstock (128). Gardens Hotel/Media.fla-keys (140). **Chapter 7: Gateways to the Keys:** Phillip Pessar/Flickr (165). Vlad Kryhin/iStockphoto (174). **About Our Writers:** All photos are courtesy of the writers except for the following: Sara Liss courtesy of Michael Pisarri.

Every effort has been made to trace the copyright holders, and we apologize in advance for any accidental errors. We would be happy to apply the corrections in the following edition of this publication.

Fodor's InFocus FLORIDA KEYS

Publisher: Stephen Horowitz, *General Manager*

Editorial: Douglas Stallings, *Editorial Director;* Jill Fergus, Amanda Sadlowski, *Senior Editors;* Kayla Becker, Brian Eschrich, Alexis Kelly, *Editors;* Angelique Kennedy-Chavannes, *Assistant Editor*

Design: Tina Malaney, *Director of Design and Production;* Jessica Gonzalez, *Senior Designer;* Erin Caceres, *Graphic Design Associate*

Production: Jennifer DePrima, *Editorial Production Manager;* Elyse Rozelle, *Senior Production Editor;* Monica White, *Production Editor*

Maps: Rebecca Baer, *Senior Map Editor;* Mark Stroud (Moon Street Cartography) and David Lindroth, *Cartographers*

Photography: Viviane Teles, *Senior Photo Editor;* Namrata Aggarwal, Neha Gupta, Payal Gupta, Ashok Kumar, *Photo Editors;* Eddie Aldrete, *Photo Production Intern;* Kadeem McPherson, *Photo Production Associate Intern*

Business and Operations: Chuck Hoover, *Chief Marketing Officer;* Robert Ames, *Group General Manager*

Public Relations and Marketing: Joe Ewaskiw, *Senior Director of Communications and Public Relations*

Fodors.com: Jeremy Tarr, *Editorial Director;* Rachael Levitt, *Managing Editor*

Technology: Jon Atkinson, *Director of Technology;* Rudresh Teotia, *Associate Director of Technology;* Alison Lieu, *Project Manager*

Writer: Sara Liss

Editor: Laura M. Kidder

Production Editor: Jennifer DePrima

Copyright © 2023 by Fodor's Travel, a division of MH Sub I, LLC, dba Internet Brands.

Fodor's is a registered trademark of Internet Brands, Inc. All rights reserved. Published in the United States by Fodor's Travel, a division of Internet Brands, Inc. No maps, illustrations, or other portions of this book may be reproduced in any form without written permission from the publisher.

8th edition

ISBN 978-1-64097-567-5

ISSN 1942-7328

All details in this book are based on information supplied to us at press time. Always confirm information when it matters, especially if you're making a detour to visit a specific place. Fodor's expressly disclaims any liability, loss, or risk, personal or otherwise, that is incurred as a consequence of the use of any of the contents of this book.

SPECIAL SALES

This book is available at special discounts for bulk purchases for sales promotions or premiums. For more information, e-mail SpecialMarkets@fodors.com.

PRINTED IN CANADA

10 9 8 7 6 5 4 3 2 1

About Our Writer

 Sara Liss is a Miami-based food and travel writer. Well traveled and trilingual in English, Hebrew, and Farsi, Liss started her career in journalism in the Middle East, where she was a reporter for the Associated Press's Jerusalem bureau and *Time Out Istanbul*. She moved to South Florida in 2003 and has contributed to a wide range of publications, including *Condé Nast Traveler*, *The Miami Herald*, *Departures*, and *MIAMI Modern Luxury*. In order to update all the chapters for the *In Focus Florida Keys* guidebook, she took a deep dive into Keys life, consuming many key lime pie slices, margaritas, and fish sandwiches! Her first cookbook, *Miami Cooks*, featuring recipes from the city's best restaurants, was released in the fall of 2020. She resides in Surfside near Miami Beach with her husband and three kids. Follow her on Instagram *@Slissmia*.